TAMING TIME

TAMING TIME

or

HOW DO YOU EAT AN ELEPHANT?

Planning for success:

Improve your time-management skills
An instructional handbook for improving time-management
and self-management skills, using the TIMETECH system

Gary Kroehnert

The McGraw-Hill Companies, Inc.

Sydney New York San Francisco Auckland
Bangkok Bogotá Caracas Hong Kong
Kuala Lumpur Lisbon London Madrid
Mexico City Milan New Delhi San Juan
Seoul Singapore Taipei Toronto

McGraw·Hill Australia

A Division of The **McGraw·Hill** Companies

Reprinted 2000

National Library of Australia Cataloguing-in-Publication data:

Kroehnert, Gary.
Taming time: how do you eat an elephant?: planning for success with improved time management skills.

Includes index.
ISBN 0 07 470662 4.

1. Time management. I. Title.
650.1

Published in Australia by
McGraw-Hill Book Company Australia Pty Limited
4 Barcoo Street, Roseville NSW 2069, Australia
Acquisitions Editor: Kristen Baragwanath
Production Editors: Sybil Kesteven, Felicity Shea
Designer: RTJ Klinkhamer
Cover design: RTJ Klinkhamer
Illustrator: Loui Silvestro
Typeset in 10/14 pt Janson by RTJ Klinkhamer
Printed on 80 gsm offset by Best-tri Printing & Packing Co Ltd, Hong Kong

Contents

Dedication

This book is written for, and dedicated to,
the many hundreds of thousands of young and old people
around the world who find they never have enough time.

If you're reading this book, you probably need to!
Think about it.

A special
thank you

I would like to thank the many tens of thousands of people who have attended my seminars all over the world for their input, along with the many successful people and organisations who have given me some of their time and many of their great ideas. While I will be sharing ideas with you from these famous people and businesses, some of the best time-management ideas come from people who are not famous, but from the people who share their ideas with me at my seminars.

We should all thank the many hundreds of authors who have given thousands of ideas in regard to better time-management skills. While most authors and time-management experts now talk about fourth-generation time-management skills, this book looks at an imaginary fifth generation, where they all tie in together. The different 'generations' of time management are summarised on page 189 for your reference.

Also to be thanked is Peter Sharpe from Day-Timers, along with his terrific team, for the support they have offered me over the years; also Day-Timers themselves, for their permission to use some of the material from the original Time Power seminar and the opportunity to show some of their page formats used throughout this book.

Special thanks must go to Dr Charles Hobbs, the creator of the original Time Power seminar back in the early 1970s. The Time Power seminar is the most popular time-management seminar around the world, having had well over a million people attend. Further information on the Time Power seminar can be found on page 198.

A sincere 'thank you' to all of you.

Dr Gary Kroehnert
August 1998

Introduction

(and a few personal insights)

NOTES

You may be wondering what the question on the title page is all about—how *do* you eat an elephant? What do elephants have to do with time-management skills, anyway?

Obviously, if you're going to eat an elephant, you eat it one bite at a time! It needs to be cut into small pieces so that each piece can be eaten one at a time and digested before the next bite is taken.

But how does eating elephants have anything to do with time-management skills? The answer to that question is in the fact that most things must be broken into smaller digestible chunks for processing. This book will give you some ideas on how to break things down into smaller pieces and also, importantly, to see whether it's elephants you really want to eat.

The main reason most people do not achieve all their goals is that they look at a goal and say to themselves that they haven't got time to do that right now, or that the goal is simply too large to deal with at the moment. Most people don't break their goals into smaller pieces so that the pieces can be dealt with one at a time— the same way that we should eat elephants!

In recent decades we have seen a dramatic reduction in the number of work hours in the week. Currently most people these days only spend about 1610 of the 8760 hours in the year at work (less than one hour in five).

Over this period of time we have also seen a massive increase in the number of time-saving devices available to us, such as automobiles, calculators, dishwashers, telephones, microwave ovens, automatic washing machines, electric razors, fax machines, jet aircraft, electronic mail, takeaway foods and computers. All these items allow us to do things in a fraction of the time it would have taken us a few decades ago. Yet the result of all this isn't as predicted. We don't have more time available to us and we still feel as stressed as we did before, or even more so.

It is currently estimated that well over 10 per cent of the average person's time is taken up each day watching television. This amounts to more than two and a half hours each day. How many people do you know who say they haven't got enough time these days to work towards their long-range goals? How many don't have the time to read the books they would like to read, or enough time to spend with their children? How many say they haven't enough time to spend on recreational activities, or to get involved in other leisure activities?

Maybe it's just a matter of turning the television off a little sooner, or getting out of bed a little earlier sometimes so we can work towards other goals. This is not inferring that television is the cause of our problems; it's simply demonstrating that people don't always do what they value most.

Everybody has the same amount of time. Some people just prefer to invest their time in different areas. Rather than watching two and a half hours of television each day, or spending ten hours in bed, some people would rather spend time

working towards their long-range goals (which might include some time watching television). Others would prefer to spend the extra time reading, or with their children. Others would prefer to participate in recreational activities, or a wider range of leisure activities. I think you get the meaning.

It's too easy to think of tangible items such as houses, computers, cars or televisions as having a value to us. Because it's invisible to us, we don't consider time to be so important to us. If you lost your computer you would report it to the police, but if you lose some of your time, you don't even think about it. We must treat time as our most valuable resource—it's not replaceable. Once it's gone, it's gone! We can't claim it on our insurance, and it can never be given back to us. You will see further on in this book how much your time is worth in a tangible format, in dollars and cents; and just remember, it's your pocket the money is coming from.

People have a fascination with time. It's estimated that there are over 500 million watches produced every year! The watch is one of the most produced items in the world today.

Decades ago, when staff used to work very long hours, the boss was the only person who controlled what the worker did in the workplace. Times have certainly changed. Employees don't have to work the same long hours, and it's not the boss who determines exactly what needs to be done every minute of the working day. Now it's the employees who are responsible for controlling what they do in the workplace. And now that we have more leisure time available to us, we need to make sure we make effective use of it too.

In *Alice's Adventures in Wonderland*, Alice meets the Cheshire Cat, which is sitting in a tree, and asks:

> *'Cheshire Puss . . . would you tell me, please, which way I ought to go from here?'*
>
> *'That depends a good deal on where you want to get to,' said the Cat.*

What happened to Alice happens to most people all through their lives. They come to a fork in the road or a crossroad and they really don't know which way to go. Unless we are working towards clearly defined goals, it won't matter which way we go. We're going to finish up somewhere, but maybe further down the road we'll realise it isn't where we wanted to be after all.

We must have goals to help us make decisions. This book will show you how to set realistic goals for yourself. It will also show you how to find the time to work towards those goals.

Some people, when they think about time-management, think that it's a matter of 'head down and backside up' 24 hours a day. That's not what time-management is about.

When we talk about time-management we can see that we have two major responsibilities. Our first responsibility is to get a task done. The second responsibility is to look after the people. So from a time-management point of view there is absolutely nothing wrong in socialising. There is absolutely nothing wrong with stopping what we're doing, getting a cup of coffee and looking at the view from the window for ten minutes—as long as we're making conscious decisions on what we're doing.

How many times have you seen someone you know sitting at their desk, or somewhere else, working on an important project. They see out of the very corner of their eye their empty coffee cup. They automatically grab the empty cup, stand up, go over to the coffee machine and fill it up. They may not have even felt like a cup of coffee but, well, the cup was empty.

They start walking back to their office when they see a work colleague they haven't spoken to for a few days. So they go up to them and ask what's been happening. Several minutes or more pass. The coffee has gone a little cold now, so they take it back to the coffee machine and top it up. They start walking back to their office again.

They are almost back to their office when they notice someone else. They have heard that this person is going somewhere really nice for their holidays next week, so over they go to find out exactly where they're going, and all the details of the trip. And so the day goes.

Finally this person gets back to their office and they see that it's just about time to go home. 'Can't do much of this important project before knock-off time', so maybe they'll do one or two small low-priority jobs just to fill in the time. This goes on for the whole week.

This person gets to the end of the week and can't understand why the important project they planned to start on Monday is still sitting in the middle of their desk, basically untouched.

Have you ever seen this happen to other people? I'm certain it wouldn't happen to you . . . would it?

Office timetable

9.00	Official start time
9.30	Arrive at work
9.45	Morning tea
11.00	Start work
11.15	Get ready for lunch
12.00	Lunch
2.45	Restart work
3.00	Afternoon tea
4.00	Prepare to leave
4.30	Leave
5.00	Official finish time

Let's look at another person we know. This time it's the weekend. They get out of bed on Sunday morning, walk into the bathroom, brush their teeth, have a shower, get dressed and walk outside.

They open their front door, and what they see first is generally what they do first. They look out at the yard, and see that the grass is far too long. So without even thinking they go to the garage, get the mower out and start mowing the lawns.

Out of habit, when the lawns are finished, this person puts the mower away. They get the edger out and start doing the edges. While doing the edges this person notices there are a few weeds in the garden, so as soon as the edges are finished and the edger is put away they go back and start weeding the garden. Weeds are being torn out from all over. All the weeds are now out of the garden, but now look at the footpath.

They see now that the footpath is covered with the

weeds they just pulled out of the garden. So they go to the garage again and get the broom. They start sweeping the path. All the weeds are now gone but they notice that there is still a lot of dirt sitting on the footpath. So they put the broom away, go around to the side of the house and get the hose. They start hosing the footpath. And so the story goes.

This person gets to Sunday night, they know they've been busy all day and they feel pretty exhausted. But all of a sudden they realise that the most important things were overlooked. Perhaps the most important thing for that person to do on their day off was to spend some more time with their children.

So what they should be doing to avoid that situation is to sit down on Sunday morning and work out what needs to be done. After completing the list they then need to put realistic priorities on that list. They then should start working their way through the priorities. That way, when they get to Sunday night they feel just as exhausted as they did the other way, but now they know that they have been working towards their highest priorities and not generally reacting to the visual priorities (generally lower ones) that they see during the day.

Watch your thoughts; they become your words.
Watch your words; they become your actions.
Watch your actions; they become your habits.
Watch your habits; they become your destiny.

If there's one thing we need to do to be successful with the use of our time, it's to plan. So what's a reasonable definition of planning?

Planning is to identify future events and bring them into the present so that we can do something about them now.

That's not to say that we can control everything. But you'll be surprised how much control and influence we can have over most things if we go through the process the right way.

How to gain from this book

'Christmas is almost here again and I still haven't bought any presents!'

'The picnic is on tomorrow and I still have to get the food!'

'Our holidays start in two weeks and we haven't even thought about what to do yet!'

'They used to be great friends, but we haven't seen them in ages.'

'The barbecue is on tonight and we still have to buy the meat!'

'The project starts tomorrow and we still have to decide on what needs to be done first!'

'They will be here in twenty minutes and we haven't started to get ready!'

'The game starts in fifteen minutes and we still haven't decided on our positions!'

'They were babies and then all of a sudden they were grown up. What happened to the time?'

6

Do any of these statements sound familiar? I bet they do. Most people tend to put things off to the last minute. The unfortunate thing is that this tends to increase stress levels and therefore create more disorganisation, which in turn leads to higher stress levels, and so on. The good news is that it is relatively easy to learn new skills to control these situations. All it will take is a little of your reading time and some practice. Of course, I'm assuming that there is already a commitment on your part and some motivation to do it. Because without the commitment or motivation, it won't work!

A lack of time is the most common complaint people have these days in the industrialised countries. This book won't be able to give you more time, but what it will do is show you how to make better use of the time you have available to you. When you get to the end of the day, the end of the year, or the end of your life, you should be able to say to yourself that you have made the best possible use of your time over that period.

Why are good time-management skills important to us?

- They help establish a balance between our business, family and social lives.
- They help to improve quality.
- They help in the decision-making process.
- They help to control the information explosion.
- They help in overcoming procrastination.
- They improve our leadership and management skills.
- They help balance the demands placed on us by our customers.
- They help us to achieve our goals.
- They help us to become successful.

Effective use of time-management skills will make or break your career. They will also have a tremendous impact on you outside the workplace.

In recent times human beings have found ways of exploring, controlling or improving many things. Communications, travel, space and the earth are just a few areas. Now we need to move into the next frontier—ourselves! This is our greatest and most immediate challenge.

I have kept this book relatively short so as not to take too much of your valuable time. Take plenty of notes as you go along; it will help cement the ideas. Be an active reader and read with a pen or pencil in hand. Make plenty of notes at the side, top and bottom of the pages as you read through. If you like, use a bright-coloured highlighter to highlight those parts that you may like to refer to again later on. At the end of each chapter have a period of time for reflection and look for ideas that may be of assistance to you.

As you work through this book, I suggest that every time you get an idea to make better use of your time you turn to pages 177–84 and make a note of those ideas, or transfer your important notes taken on the pages as you finish each chapter. These ten pages have been set aside for your use, so please make sure you use them! It will be much easier for you if all these ideas are kept together. These few pages with your notes on them will finish up being the most important area in your handbook. Some of the ideas may seem too simple. Don't dismiss them, because simple ideas are often the best.

First, though, quickly scan through the pages so that you can see what's in store for you.

You will find, scattered through the readings, a number of exercises, quizzes and activities. I strongly suggest that all of these be completed as you go through the book. Don't think to yourself, 'I'll come back and do that later', or 'I haven't got time to do it right now', because you know and I know that you probably won't! Don't put it off.

Research indicates that if you don't take immediate action you will have forgotten 75 per cent of what you learned from this book within 24 hours, and that 96 per cent will be forgotten within 14 days. I'm looking for action from you now. If you put nothing in, you'll get nothing out!

I hear and I forget.
I see and I remember.
I do and I understand.
Confucius (c. 450 BC)

Our goals for you to achieve while working through this book are for you to:

• have a better awareness of the value of more effectively managing your time
• write your own clearly defined time-management goals
• develop a system for writing personal life goals and goals at work
• develop a system for planning and control in carrying out those goals;

and after you finish reading:

• carry out your time-management goals!

Here are a couple of things to get you started. Please take some time to fill the boxes in.

This book has some terrific ideas written in it by the owner.

The owner's name is:

_____

If found please return to:

_____

_____

_____

_____

or call on:

_____

Three things I would like to achieve from reading this book are:

1.

_____

_____

_____

_____

2.

_____

_____

_____

_____

3.

_____

_____

_____

_____

'When opportunity knocks, don't complain about the noise.'

Before you go any further, please look back at the three goals you have just identified and ask yourself if they are achievable. If they are, please continue. If they're not, go back and make any necessary modifications. If you set unrealistic goals for yourself it will decrease your motivation to keep going. You will get much more information further into this book on how to set goals, and how to achieve them.

This book is for everyone. Whether you're a butcher, baker or candlestick maker, manager, supervisor, council worker, doctor, public servant, teacher, author, production line worker, sportsperson, miner, student, politician, pilot, actor, police officer, singer, taxi driver, university lecturer, office cleaner, musician, student, mechanic, computer operator or house spouse, everyone can benefit from improved time-management techniques. And this is not limited just to people in the workplace, or just to people with a task to perform.

I would like to welcome you, not only to this book, but perhaps to a whole new way of thinking—a way of thinking that will allow you to achieve the kinds of things you would like to achieve.

This book offers ideas for possible use by the reader. Most of the ideas offered will work for most people, but there are some ideas that may not work for others. People and situations are always different. It's your choice in selecting and implementing any of these ideas. But try not to say to yourself, 'That won't work for me'. Instead, try saying, 'That won't work for me the way it's put forward, but how can I modify this idea to suit my specific situation?'

'How do you eat an elephant' will show you what the TIMETECH system is. TIMETECH is a high-performance system designed to increase your personal productivity. Its strategy is to develop a 'how to do it' approach to time-management and some of your time-management problems.

The approach is based on many successful and worthwhile ideas. As I stated in my 'special thank you', the following ideas have been gained from many successful speakers and authors around the world and from the many tens of thousands of people attending my seminars. These ideas have worked for them, so why shouldn't they work for you?

As mentioned before, many of the ideas offered may seem too simple. Don't reject these ideas because they don't sound complicated or demanding. Remember, often the best idea is the simplest!

Here's a question for you to think about.

Question: What do successful, wealthy, famous, powerful and happy people all have in common?

Answer: *They all have 86 400 seconds every day—exactly the same as everyone else. The thing they do differently, though, is to make effective use of those seconds. Other people don't!*

Imagine there is a bank that credits your account each morning with $86 400 and it carries over NO balance from day to day. At midnight every day the bank deletes whatever part of the balance you failed to use during the day. What would you do? Draw out every cent each day, of course!

Each of us has such a bank. Its name is TIME. Every morning it credits you with 86 400 seconds. Every night it writes off whatever of this you have failed to invest. It carries over no balance; it allows no overdraft. Each day it opens a new account for you; each night it burns the remains of each day. If you fail to use the day's deposits, the loss is yours. There is no going back. There is no drawing against tomorrow. You must live in the present on today's deposits. Invest it so as to get the utmost in health, happiness and success. The clock is running. Make the most of today.

To realise the value of one year, ask a student who failed a grade. To realise the value of one month, ask a mother who gave birth to a premature baby. To realise the value of one week, ask the editor of a weekly paper. To realise the value of one hour, ask the lovers who are waiting to meet. To realise the value of one minute, ask the person who just missed their train. To realise the value of one second, ask the person who just avoided an accident. To realise the value of one millisecond, ask the person who won a silver medal in the Olympics.

Treasure every moment you have! And treasure it more because you shared it with someone special—special enough to spend your time. And remember that time waits for no-one. Yesterday is history, tomorrow is a mystery. Today is a gift. That's why it's called the present!

I also suggest that you think about other people's needs as you work through this book. If you can organise other people around you more effectively, both in the workplace and outside the workplace, I think you will agree that it makes it much easier for you to organise yourself. So pass on lots of ideas to them.

Keep asking yourself how these ideas can apply to you. Keep asking yourself how these ideas can apply to other people around you. You need to educate other people around you.

One way of getting other people around you to organise themselves more effectively could be to buy them their own personal copy of this book! If you think this could help you, or them, you will find order forms located in the back of this book for your convenience. (It will also save you some shopping time!) There is also a request form at the back for training services—both our public seminars and in-house training services— and there is some information on 'personal organisers'.

As this is a book based on time-management, we should now look at the real definition of what time-management is.

What is time management?

Before we look at the definition of time management, we need to think about what we limit time-management skills to. Improving our organisational skills? Making more money? Improving communication? Having better sales figures? Getting better grades with our studies?

NOTES

As we will be looking at a system of improved time-management skills we need to understand what the basic definition of time management is.

Let's break the term into its two separate components. We will look at the words 'time' and 'management' separately.

The term 'time' is used on many occasions during the day by most people. But, unfortunately, most do not stop and think about this frequently-used term. Over the years many definitions have been put forward by many well-respected sources, such as Kant, Drucker, Augustine and Einstein.

When St Augustine was writing about time, he said, 'What is time? If no-one asks me I know. But if I'm asked by a questioner I don't know'. This is certainly true of most people. We think we know what we mean by the term 'time', but not too many of us ever sit down and think about what we really mean by it.

Peter Drucker, a well-respected American management consultant, states that time is our scarcest resource, and unless it is managed nothing else can be managed. Obviously Drucker isn't suggesting that we can manage time, as we all know that time is an inflexible state. Strictly speaking, the term 'time management' is a misnomer. The correct term should be 'self-management'. We cannot manage time itself, but what we can do is manage ourselves more effectively.

Albert Einstein concluded that time was the occurrence of events one after another, and this is now the generally accepted definition. You may be saying to yourself that there are some events occurring at the same time, but when you look at the real term of 'self-management', we as individuals can focus only on one

given event at any one period in time. That may just be for a fraction of a second, and we keep going backwards and forwards between those events.

Please take a minute to write your definition of time.

Time is:

_____

_____

_____

_____

I've asked many thousands of people, as clients of mine, what they mean by the term 'time'. I've also asked many thousands of my seminar attendees what they expect to find in a time-management seminar. It's not very often that people can answer these questions off the top of their head.

When I ask people in time-management seminars to put forward a definition of 'time', the more common responses include the following:

- Time is a constant.
- Time is money.
- Time is a measure.
- Time is a period of space.
- Time is a measure designed by humans.
- Time is a period of space to get things done.
- Time is a period of space not to get things done.

- Time is the missing dimension.
- Time is the only thing that stops everything happening at once.

Some people ask me to give them extra hours during the day so that they can get more things done! I have both good news and bad news for people making that request. The good news is that the earth's rotation is slowing down and the days are gradually getting longer. World time is slowing down by approximately one-thousandth of a second per day according to our atomic clock. Therefore (without modification) in just over 9800 years we will have a 25-hour day! That's the good news. The bad news is that most people can't afford to wait that long. Can you really afford to wait that long? I don't think so. We have to make more productive use of the time we have available right now.

By far the best definition I've had put forward so far is the age-old saying, 'Time is life'. If we look at this type of definition we can see that if we waste any of our time we are wasting our lives. And unlike most things, we can't save time to be used at a later date. As the clock ticks, not only are the seconds disappearing, but so is our life. Once it's past, it's gone for ever!

People talk about 'gaining time' or 'losing time', but neither of these terms is true. We cannot gain time or lose time. We all have set amounts—no more or no less. What we should be doing is planning our time more effectively so that we are starting to control it.

Regardless of whether we are rich or poor, bright or stupid, we all have the same amount of time available to us. All resources are designed to be used, including time. But time differs a little from other resources. It is the only one that is non-renewable, neither is it recyclable. It is also the only one that is distributed in equal measure to each of us. No-one has more or less than anyone else. However, some people manage to make far better use of the time available to them. Most people these days need to find ways of utilising their time more effectively.

Most people have to stop and think about the term 'time'. This means that most people really don't know what to expect when attending a 'time-management' seminar, or perhaps what to expect from reading a book on 'time management'.

Now let's look at the term 'management'. The generally accepted definition of management these days is: 'Management is the act of controlling relevant events in an effective manner'. From this statement we can make a couple of fairly safe assumptions. If we are managing something well, we can assume that this thing is under control. We can also assume that if we are not managing something well it is probably out of control.

When we put both of these definitions together we can see that the real definition of the term 'time management' would be:

 Time management is the act of controlling relevant events in the most effective way.

To carry this a little further we could say that:

 Time management, or self-management, is the act of controlling relevant events by maximising time and talents to achieve worthwhile goals based on a sound values system.

Time is everything!

If we cannot improve our time-management or self-management skills it will result in:

- rushing around
- chronically putting things off
- being unable to decide between unpleasant alternatives
- missing deadlines
- insufficient time for rest
- insufficient time for personal relationships
- the sense of being overwhelmed by demands and details
- the feeling that you do what you don't want to do most of the time.

I'd like to give you some information on a research project that was carried out a few years ago. The researchers wanted to find out which profession lived the longest. They did!

Some people suggest that the average male these days lives to 78 years of age, and the average female lives to 80 years of age. In contrast, the profession they found to live longest has an average life expectancy of 87 years of age. Which profession do you think lives longer than all others? Take a minute to think about it.

The more common suggestions include professions such as religious people, people from the horizontal leisure profession, gardeners, house spouses, teachers . . . some people even suggest time-management consultants! So which profession lives longer than others? Symphony orchestra conductors! Conductors of symphony orchestras live longer than other people.

The researchers went in to find out why they live longer than other professions. There were a number of suggestions and explanations as to why this is so, but the ones we're interested in right now are based on the fact that these people have control over things, and therefore have lower stress levels.

The main point in telling this story is to show that people in some professions typically live longer than those in other professions, and therefore people in some professions have a shorter life. The question right now is, 'Where would your profession fall on a scale of 1 to 10?'

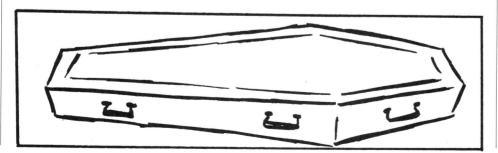

Maybe now you can see some really long-term implications from reading and working through this book. If you can find some ways of controlling things around you a little more effectively, maybe you can move up a couple of points on the scale—who knows?

What are three problems you currently encounter with poor time-management skills?

1.

_____

_____

_____

_____

2.

_____

_____

_____

_____

3.

_____

_____

_____

_____

An error doesn't become a mistake until you refuse to correct it.

It will take time to master these new skills. How much time? The time required to master new skills will be somewhere between 6 weeks and 6 months, depending on the person and their motivation to want to change. Most people these days see change as a threat, and therefore avoid it as much as they possibly can. We should look at change as being an incredible opportunity to master new and more interesting skills. With these new skills we will find a greater sense of achievement, an increase in self-esteem, a greater sense of awareness, lower stress levels, more time to spend on more pleasurable activities, and so on. The list goes on.

So here is that question again: what do we limit time-management skills to? Improving our organisational skills? Making more money? Improving communication? Having better sales figures? Getting better grades with our studies? The answer is—all of the above plus everything else! Everything we do, think, or feel has something to do with our time. So any improvement anywhere will be a step in the right direction towards improving our time-management skills.

This isn't suggesting that we can control all events around us. We can control only the ones that are controllable. When we talk about controlling events, there are three major conditions that need to be considered, as we shall see in the next chapter.

Conditions of controlling events

(NOTES)

When we talk about or look at controlling events, we need also to consider three conditions that are involved. These are all equally important and should all be recognised.

Condition number 1 of controlling events suggests that there are events that are uncontrollable. These are events over which we have literally no control. Examples of events like this are:

- weather conditions
- acts of God
- traffic jams.

List three more events that are completely beyond your control:

1.

2.

3.

Condition number 2 of controlling events suggests that there are events that involve other people's behaviour. These are events over which we have indirect control.

If we are to have some control over events that involve other people's behaviour we need to influence others. Some examples are:

• the ringing telephone
• people coming into your office
• absenteeism.

List three more events that can be controlled by influencing others around us:

1.

_____

_____

2.

_____

_____

3.

_____

_____

Condition number 3 of controlling events suggests that there are events that involve our own behaviour. These are events over which we have direct control.

Examples of events that involve our own behaviour and therefore are controllable are:

- getting ready for work on time
- doing things when they need to be done
- being more assertive.

List three more events that can be controlled by changing our behaviour:

1.

2.

3.

We can see that both condition number 2 events and condition number 3 events are controllable. They are controllable either by changing our own habits or by influencing other people's habits. Condition number 1 events are literally beyond our control. However, once we can identify an event that is literally beyond our control we should then be looking at ways of adapting to that situation.

The traffic jam was used above as an example of an event that is beyond our control—a condition number 1. Some people would argue that it is controllable, because we could always leave early to make sure we reach where we are going on time. That's not really controlling the situation. What it is doing is adapting to the situation.

We hear on the radio in the morning that there is a traffic jam somewhere, or that there has been an accident somewhere. What we then do is to leave a little earlier, to make sure we get to where we are going on time. Or we might adapt by going around the affected area, again to make sure we get to where we are going on time. This is adapting, not controlling!

Any time you can identify an event that is literally beyond your control, don't look for ways of controlling it. Instead, look for ways of adapting to that event. Keep your stress levels down. It's pointless getting stressed over events that are beyond your control.

Condition number 2 identifies most interruptions we have. Condition number 2 suggested that there are events that involve other people's behaviour, not ours.

People think that there is nothing they can do about the phone ringing all the time. They think there is nothing they can do about people knocking on their door all the time, or coming into their office, or dumping more work on their desk. But when we stop and think about it, there are probably quite a few ideas that could be used to start controlling these interruptions.

Condition number 2 tends to highlight the fact that most people are not assertive enough. How often do you get to the end of the day and look at your desk, only to find it still covered with projects that you haven't started yet? You think to yourself, 'Why did I say I would do all of those things?'

Maybe what some people need to do is to put their hand up a little more frequently during the day and say to others, 'I'm too busy' or, 'I'm working on something else that's really important'. If you can't put your hand up to that person, the event may be a condition number 1. In that case it's an event that we cannot control. What we should be doing is looking for ways of adapting, and therefore keeping our stress levels down.

Condition number 3 suggested that there are events that involve our own behaviour, not others'. This really focuses in on procrastination and rationalisation, as well as touching on a number of other areas. This is the area over which we have most control. Condition number 3 is normally the main reason why people turn up on a voluntary basis to time-management programs. Most people know that they keep putting off until tomorrow what should be done today.

Condition number 3 also shows us that we cannot control everyone around us. There is only one person we can control all of the time, and that's ourselves.

This statement summarises the three conditions:

 If you don't have the ability to control your life, you will have to accept the fact that life controls you!

Please take any ideas you may now have to pages 177–84.

Balance

NOTES

When we consider controlling events in our lives, we also need to look at the balance or range of events happening around us. These are the things that we need to consider and make sure we get involved in.

This balance includes all the things we should be getting involved in at the workplace, all the things we should be getting involved with at home, and all the other things that we are involved with, such as sports, exercise, friends, studies, hobbies, leisure activities and so on.

When people start approaching their 'use by' date, how often do you think they sit back and ask themselves, 'If I had my time over again, what would I do differently?' Most people think this way at some stage in their lives.

In a recent survey conducted with people in the 80-plus age group, the individuals were all asked the question shown above. Almost without exception, every person responded by saying that they would spend more time with their children while they were younger, or spend more time with their friends or other family members.

What these people were doing was reflecting on what they had done with their lives. It's an unfortunate state of affairs when people focus only on their work responsibilities. They also have responsibilities in other areas. Don't get to your 'use by' date and realise this when it's too late to do anything about it.

How can you obtain, or simply maintain, a balance of things around you? There are a number of considerations to take into account. Some of the tasks that have to be done to obtain or maintain a better balance include:

- setting clearly defined goals
- achieving goals
- understanding your values
- being able to retrieve information instantly and accurately
- never losing any useful idea
- communicating effectively with others.

Setting clearly defined goals

Setting clearly defined goals in the right kinds of categories (both personal and professional) gets you to look at the categories that need to be considered for a balanced planning of goals. Unfortunately, most people don't cover all of their bases, which throws them out of balance very quickly.

Achieving goals

If you can get to the end of the day, month or year, and tick off your goals as being achieved, it shows that you have been working towards your clearly defined goals. However, there are many successful people who have never really achieved any of their long-range goals. Goal achievement isn't necessarily success in itself. My definition of success is shown towards the end of this book.

Understanding your values

Understanding your personal values will form the basis of your goal-setting process. Personal values are the basis of the goal-setting process and help us make important decisions.

Being able to retrieve information instantly and accurately

The information you need to retrieve can link in with the goals you are setting yourself. It's important to have the ability to access information instantly and accurately. You will see how this can be done when we look at the correct way of using an organiser.

Never losing any useful idea

The ideas that you generate during the day can again link in with the clearly defined goals you are setting for yourself. Because this is so important, we will also look at a way of using an organiser so that you never lose those useful ideas again.

Communicating effectively with others

If there is one thing that will throw a person out of balance very quickly, it's poor communication, or lack of it. If you don't know what other people expect of you, or they don't know what you expect of them, you could be working on the wrong issues. And from a time-management point of view, it doesn't make much sense doing a job the right way if you're doing the wrong job in the first place.

If you can say to yourself at any stage while going through this book that poor communication or lack of communication is a significant time-management problem for you, then I suggest that you turn to page 165 and write yourself a goal to look at improving communication in the appropriate area or with the appropriate person. Poor communication isn't a time-management problem—it's a pure management problem.

Do you need to improve on any of these areas?

	yes	no
	(please tick)	
setting clearly defined goals	☐	☐
achieving goals	☐	☐
understanding one's values	☐	☐
retrieving information instantly and accurately	☐	☐
never losing any useful idea	☐	☐
communicating effectively with others	☐	☐

Hold your child's hand every time you get the chance. The time will come when he or she won't let you.

Exercise to increase productivity

NOTES

We do not stop playing because we are old; we grow old because we stop playing.

If I had known I was going to live this long I would have taken better care of myself.

Some people think exercise is having a bath, pulling the plug, and fighting the current. Other people get winded just jumping to conclusions!

It has been found that people who exercise regularly will actually become more productive during the day. There are those who say that exercise will drain your energy and leave you exhausted, but that only applies for those who exercise to extreme.

Regular exercise in moderation will increase your energy level. While exercising, your body produces adrenalin and endorphins. Adrenalin helps to keep you going, while the endorphins are the body's natural painkiller, believed to be fifty times more powerful than morphine.

Regular exercise will improve your ability to concentrate. It will improve the clarity of your thinking, and it will improve your energy levels. There are many benefits.

Set up an exercise program for yourself of, say, 30 minutes three times per week—every Monday, Wednesday and Friday. The type of exercise will very much depend on what you like doing, what your friends do, and your current level of health.

For your exercise program, you should consult someone who is appropriately qualified in this area to give you specific advice regarding your needs and requirements.

What should I do to increase my level of energy?

_____

_____

_____

_____

_____

_____

Time-wasters

There are literally thousands of time-wasters around us. These time-wasters are the things that stop us from doing the really important things. Some of them are very obvious, some of them not so obvious. Listed below are the typical, more common types of time-wasters identified by seminar participants:

- not delegating things that should be
- using poor delegation skills
- going off on tangents all the time
- not assessing results
- procrastination—putting things off
- too many meetings
- ineffective meetings
- having an unrealistic work plan
- not understanding your job
- not understanding the task
- not understanding your role
- not listening to other people
- trying to do everything yourself
- over-planning
- under-planning
- doing too many things at once
- an inability to deal with interruptions
- not sticking to deadlines
- setting unrealistic deadlines
- not trusting other people
- having an unorganised workplace
- private matters at work
- not concentrating on results
- implementing temporary fixes
- uncontrolled telephone calls
- lack of morale
- taking inappropriate short cuts
- not having set priorities
- stopping other people from working
- not doing first things first
- not using a diary effectively
- using incorrect priorities
- poor arrangement of appointments
- inappropriate attention to detail
- socialising too much in the workplace
- poor communications
- not completing anything at all
- avoiding your responsibilities
- not thinking enough
- changing plans without notice
- making too many snap decisions
- not getting it right first time
- trying to be involved in everything
- being disorganised
- not following through with decisions
- having a cluttered desk
- too many newspapers and magazines
- trying to please everyone
- doing too many favours for others
- not being able to say 'no'
- watching too much television
- trying to create impressions
- looking at effort rather than results

- having untrained staff
- not keeping appropriate records
- a feeling of panic
- too much commuting time

- lacking motivation
- doing things too quickly (mistakes)
- futzing* (definition shown below)
- the list goes on, and on . . .

* So what's 'futzing'? This term is used to describe what people are doing when wasting time on computers. Futzing is spending 70 minutes deciding which font to use. Futzing is spending 95 minutes setting up the background colours for your screen. These examples assume that spending all that time selecting fonts or colours isn't important; if it is important, it's not a waste of time. Futzing takes you away from the really important items. It's a great modern-day way to procrastinate!

What are five time-wasters you can identify for yourself in the workplace?

1.

2.

3.

4.

5.

What are five time-wasters you can identify for yourself outside the workplace?

1.

_____

_____

2.

_____

_____

3.

_____

_____

4.

_____

_____

5.

_____

_____

As you read through this book, I would like you to keep the ten items shown above in the back of your mind. Every time you come across an idea to control one of those time-wasters, take the idea over to pages 177–84 and write them down. You will need the ideas written on these pages for a very important activity you will be involved in later.

As mentioned earlier, some people think that time management is a matter of 'head down and backside up'. That's not the case. When we look at time management we have two major responsibilities. First, as we all know, we have the responsibility of getting the task done. Our second responsibility is to look after the people involved in the process.

So, from a time-management point of view, there is absolutely nothing wrong in socialising with people. There is also absolutely nothing wrong in taking your cup of coffee over to the window and looking at the view for 10 minutes, as long as you are making conscious decisions about what you are doing, and not reacting to the empty coffee cup as we saw earlier.

I'm sure that you don't react automatically to your empty coffee cup, but you probably know people who do. So what you need to do, in that case, is to give them a tap on the shoulder and help to bring them back in line so that they can start making conscious, proactive decisions on what needs to be done.

What is our time worth?

Many people say, 'Time is money'. Time is similar to money in some ways but not in others. For example, we can't save time the way we can money.

Let's have a quick look at what our time is really worth. The table on the following page calculates the actual hourly cost of time for people at various income levels. It's based on a 40-hour working week. The value of each of your hours, even each of your minutes, is something you should keep in mind when you review your day's activities. Look at your time as money to invest. At the end of the day, congratulate yourself for good 'investments', and also identify any bad 'investments'.

You are also 'investing' the time of people who report to you, and other people whose time you consume. Consider these costs as well.

What is your time worth per hour?

_____

What is your time worth per minute?

_____

(Keep these figures in mind; you will need them later.)

Annual salary	Weekly salary	Overheads (+40%)	Total per week	Value per hour	Value per minute
$1 000	$19	$8	$27	$1	$0.01
2 000	39	15	54	1	0.02
3 000	58	23	81	2	0.03
4 000	77	31	108	3	0.04
5 000	96	38	135	3	0.06
6 000	115	46	162	4	0.07
7 000	135	54	188	5	0.08
8 000	154	62	215	5	0.09
9 000	173	69	242	6	0.10
10 000	192	77	269	7	0.11
15 000	288	115	404	10	0.17
20 000	385	154	538	13	0.22
25 000	481	192	673	17	0.28
30 000	577	231	808	20	0.34
35 000	673	269	942	24	0.39
40 000	769	308	1 077	27	0.45
45 000	865	346	1 212	30	0.50
50 000	962	385	1 346	34	0.56
55 000	1 058	423	1 481	37	0.62
60 000	1 154	462	1 615	40	0.67
65 000	1 250	500	1 750	44	0.73
70 000	1 346	538	1 885	47	0.79
75 000	1 442	577	2 019	50	0.84
80 000	1 538	615	2 154	54	0.90
85 000	1 635	654	2 288	57	0.95
90 000	1 731	692	2 423	61	1.01
95 000	1 827	731	2 558	64	1.07
100 000	1 923	769	2 692	67	1.12
125 000	2 404	962	3 365	84	1.40
150 000	2 885	1 154	4 038	101	1.68
175 000	3 365	1 346	4 712	118	1.96
200 000	3 846	1 538	5 385	135	2.24
250 000	4 808	1 923	6 731	168	2.80
300 000	5 769	2 308	8 077	202	3.37
350 000	6 731	2 692	9 423	236	3.92
400 000	7 692	3 077	10 769	269	4.49
450 000	8 654	3 462	12 116	303	5.05
500 000	9 615	3 846	13 461	337	5.61

This chart certainly doesn't mean that you have to keep an eye on the clock while you're spending time with your spouse, children or friends, or while you're doing such things as playing sport. These things are valuable investments. Filling in the chart is simply meant to show you how valuable your time is. Nothing comes for free. Time isn't free.

You should be starting to realise by now that some of the time we spend doing certain things is really a very poor investment. These poor-investment items get done at the expense of something else—something that would give you a much greater return.

How much time did you spend reading the paper
at work today?

_____

What was that time worth? _____

Was it a good investment? _____

How much time did you spend in idle chit-chat today? _____

What was that time worth? _____

Was it a good investment? _____

How much time did you spend trying to find things today? _____

What was that time worth? _____

Was it a good investment? _____

How much time did you spend in irrelevant meetings today? _____

What was that time worth? _____

Was it a good investment? _____

How much time did you spend travelling to work today? _____

What was that time worth? _____

Was it a good investment? _____

Don't spend $50 doing a 50c job! And don't spend hours trying to find a missing 20c in the petty cash float if it's not really important to you or your position!

Identify your poor investments and then look at ways of cutting down on some of that wasted time. The 'time log' you'll be looking at later is a tool that can be used to identify all your current time-wasters.

The main point in this exercise is not to become materialistic about time, but to highlight the fact that our time is incredibly valuable. Time is a precious resource. Once it's been spent we can't get it back. So what we should do is to plan where our time will be used.

Planning your time

NOTES

Dig your well before you get thirsty!

How much time do you spend each day, on average, in high-quality planning? High-quality planning is sitting with a pen and paper in hand, planning what needs to be done today, tomorrow, next week, next year and so on, without any distractions or interruptions. Please tick the appropriate box.

Minutes spent planning	(Tick one)
0	☐
1–10	☐
11–20	☐
21–30	☐
30+	☐

By far the majority of people tick the '0' or the '1–10' boxes. It has been found that the really successful people spend more than that amount of time planning their days.

It's very difficult to say exactly how much time a person needs to put aside to plan their day, because everyone has different needs and requirements. Some people could get all their planning done in just a couple of minutes, while others might need hours to plan their day.

Some people say that they get their planning done while they are in the shower or while they are driving to work. This can be part of the planning time, but the key issue here is that after you get out of the shower and dry yourself off (and I guess put some clothes on), or when you get to work after the drive, you sit down and write

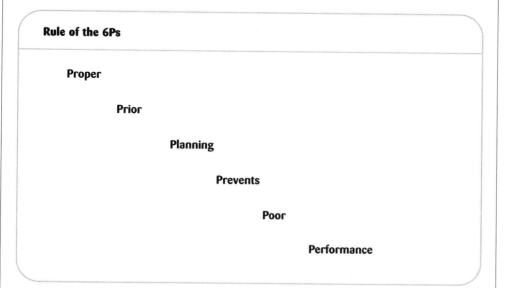
your mental plan out. That way there is far less chance of forgetting the high priorities or simply running out of time to do them. If you don't write things down, they will be forgotten!

Most people don't need to sit for 3 hours to plan a task of 2 minutes in duration, but some people do. We must make the time to set our plan in place. I suggest that the average type person these days should set aside 10–20 minutes each day to plan. This 10–20 minutes needs to be high-quality, so no distractions! Solitude is best.

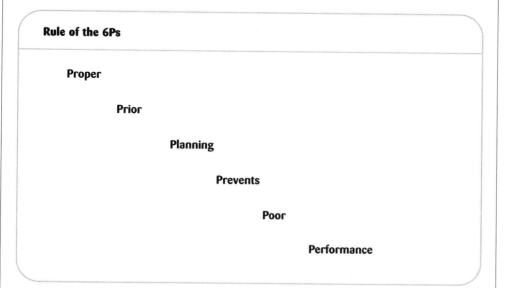

Rule of the 6Ps

     Proper

         Prior

              Planning

                  Prevents

                       Poor

                            Performance

This planning time isn't just sitting there thinking about things that need to be done today. A lot needs to happen during that planning time. You'll see how it works as we go further.

Always buy ladders, extension leads and garden hoses longer than you think you'll need.

The single most significant goal you could set yourself from reading this book is to put aside some time each day to plan your day. It's essential that you find some time. If you don't, you'll finish up in an incredibly reactive situation; and once in a reactive rut, it's very hard to get out of it.

Planning is to identify future events and bring them into the present.

I've spoken to many thousands of people over the years about planning, and asked many of them why they don't spend any time planning their day. You know what the most common response is? They say, 'I haven't got time to plan my day. I'm too busy!'

Some people get so involved in reacting to short-term urgencies that they never

get time to work towards the more important, longer-term priorities. I think you probably know what I'm talking about.

'That sounds great. I agree I should spend more time planning. But how can I find the time to do it?'

One obvious answer is to sleep less!

There have been numerous studies conducted to find out how much time a person needs to sleep. Although the findings vary, in the vast majority of cases it is found that most people sleep more than they physically require. Current research indicates that the average adult person has a requirement of between $5\frac{1}{2}$ hours and 6 hours per night.

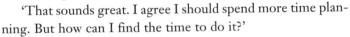

How many hours' sleep do you get during the average 24-hour day?

_____

Do you really need this much? _____

How many hours can you realistically cut this down to?

_____

If you are motivated to reduce the amount of sleep you get, here are a couple of ideas to help you. Don't cut the amount down to extreme levels in one go. The best way is to get up just 5 minutes earlier than normal in the morning for a week. The next week, get up another 5 minutes earlier; the following week another 5 minutes, and so on.

You should continue going to bed at the same time each night. After a short period of time you will find the optimum amount of sleep you require.

It has been found that the majority of people who reduce the amount of sleep they get do not continue on with this new routine. It appears that only the people who make productive use of this extra time continue on. Most people find that the work they originally had to do now expands to fill the additional waking time they now have. They finish up by not achieving more, but simply keeping themselves busier for longer each day.

To change our sleeping patterns may be only part of the solution. This additional waking time needs to be planned effectively so that it isn't simply a matter of the work expanding to take up the extra time available.

How do you make yourself get up a little earlier? Here are a few ideas for you to think about and build on.

• Move the alarm clock away from the bed so that you have to get out of bed to turn it off.

- In the middle of winter use a bright light attached to a timer and have it turn itself on when you need to get out of bed.
- Make a commitment to meet someone early in the morning, go for a run with someone, or perhaps go for a workout with someone at the gym.

Try to develop a consistent plan when looking at the broader picture. If you regularly use a monthly plan, try and use the same time each month for doing certain tasks. Maybe the first week in the month is used for visiting regular clients; maybe the second week is used for calling on new clients. The third week might be used for processing orders and proposals, and so on. I think you'll get the drift of what I mean.

While the idea of getting up a little earlier in the morning might suit the fowls, it may not suit the owls. If you're more of a night person, just adapt the ideas to suit your routine.

Please don't get me wrong. I'm not suggesting that you need to set your alarm clock for one o'clock in the morning and get up and go to work! All I'm suggesting is that we need to find time somewhere to do the things we want to do, and this is simply one of many options we can look at.

Now go over to pages 177–84 and add any ideas you may have.

Where does our time go?

You may have a swimming pool located in your backyard. How much time do you spend swimming and how much time do you spend skimming and vacuuming? You may have your own yacht. How much time do you spend sailing and how much time do you spend repairing? You may find that you are financially better off to get somebody else to do these jobs for you, or maybe even better off to sell the boat!

We have probably all known of someone who had a holiday house hidden away in the country or on the coast. How much of their time did they spend in maintaining and repairing this property? Truth be known, if they looked at the amount of time they actually spent enjoying the property they could be better off selling and investing their money. And with the return on their investment they could holiday overseas every year and still be financially better off.

Yes, it's okay for someone to spend their time maintaining these items as long as they know that they could be doing something more productive with that time if they preferred.

It takes just under 40 per cent of the total day to satisfy our perceived vital biological needs (8 hours sleeping, 2 hours eating, 1 hour dressing, personal care and hygiene): 11 hours in total. On top of this we need to be able to finance all of the above activities as well as provide housing and other needs. Therefore we need to spend time at work to earn our finances. This is about another 8 hours each day plus an hour's travelling time; say 9 hours in total. On top of this we have other routine activities such as housework and shopping; say another 2 hours each day.

So we have some 2 hours each day to devote to other activities such as leisure, sports, family, studies, entertainment and so on. If we spend another $2\frac{1}{2}$ hours watching television (as we determined earlier), we can see we don't have enough time to do anything else. In fact we are already in the red!

Something has to be done. We need to determine exactly where our time goes during the day.

Most people have had the experience of getting to the end of the day, feeling exhausted from being busy all day, but having a really hard time trying to work out where the time has gone. Has that ever happened to you?

If it has, then you need to run a log on yourself to see where your time goes during the day. A sample log has been included towards the end of this chapter for your use. Please feel free to copy this time log for yourself as often as you like.

It makes it much easier to solve a problem if we can identify exactly what the problem is. This is a basic rule that refers to any problem that needs solving. The time log will identify exactly what time-management problems you currently have.

It's like the parent showing their child a magic trick. The parent sits closely in front of the child, gets a sheet of paper out and screws it up into a ball. It's held tightly in the closed palm of the parent's hand. They tell the child that they will make it disappear. While they are telling the story they move their hands about. And at one point during the story they throw the ball of paper over the child's shoulder (so the child doesn't notice). When they open their hand the paper has 'disappeared'. The point here is that sometimes we get so close to things that we can't see the obvious. The time log will help you sit back and see the bigger picture.

With the time log you have a couple of options to think about. A time log can be run just in the workplace—from when you first get to work until you leave—or it can be run for the whole day, from when you first get out of bed until you hop back in. The choice is yours. But don't wait for a typical day to occur before you run your log. How often do you have a typical day? I suggest that there is no such thing as a typical day for most people. Every day is different for most of us.

What you need to do is run the log over a set period of time; I suggest 2 weeks (14 days). This will give you a fair indication of where your time typically goes during the day.

There are two very important rules with time logs. The first rule is that you mustn't forget about them. You can't get to the end of the day, clear your desk, then say to yourself, 'What else do I have to do before I leave?', and then answer yourself by saying, 'I've still got to fill in my time log!'. If you do that, you'll go to your top drawer and pull out this blank piece of paper, thinking to yourself, 'What on earth did I do at 8 o'clock this morning?'

If you try to fill in your time log at the end of the day, you will only remember the larger projects you were involved in. You won't remember the smaller things that happened during the day. It's very important that all of these small items be recorded, because that's by far where the bulk of our time goes, with those quick little interruptions, and so on. When you run this time log on yourself you'll soon see that these quick little interruptions weren't so quick, and that they took up a fairly significant part of the day.

Why should I run a time log on myself?

_____

_____

_____

_____

_____

When will I start it?

_____

A goal you will want to write for yourself now on page 165 could be:

Starting _____ _[date] I will run a time log on myself for the next two weeks to see where my time is currently being used._

Not everyone needs to run a time log on themselves. If you're incredibly effective with the use of your time you probably don't need to. It could, in fact, finish up wasting some of your time. But most people do need to find out where their time goes during the day. Remember the story before about the close-up magic? We need to step back occasionally. I suggest that, if you're reading this book, you will more than likely need to run a time log on yourself.

Admit to your mistakes straightaway and rectify them immediately. This will also lead to a self-correcting tendency.

 Don't wash a car, mow a yard or select a Christmas tree after dark.

Here are some categories of activities that may be included in a time log; but certainly don't limit yourself to just these:

At work
- socialising
- interruptions
- low-priority work
- finding things
- helping others
- training
- productive work
- telephone calls
- meetings — formal
- meetings — informal
- routine tasks
- administrative tasks
- sales

Outside the workplace
- telephone calls
- television
- reading
- exercise activity
- conversation
- civic activities
- commuting
- shopping
- hobbies
- daydreaming
- household chores
- childcare
- personal hygiene
- drinking
- eating
- cooking
- sexual activities
- doing nothing
- sleeping

I once heard about a Personal Assistant using a time log to prove to his boss that he was wasting a huge amount of his time on what he considered a low-priority task. The important work wasn't being completed and the boss wasn't happy or impressed.

This Personal Assistant initially found that at the end of each work day all of his important tasks weren't completed and he had to stay back late regularly to catch up. Because he had other personal commitments after normal work hours he decided that he had better find a way to fix things—and fix them quickly!

The Personal Assistant decided to keep a time log on his own work over the next week and it listed everything he did in the workplace for the next working week.

On summarising the collected information it was found that just over 4 hours during the week were devoted to getting coffee for the boss. The boss had a particular liking for the coffee made downstairs at the local cafe, and guess who had to get it for her all the time?

The Personal Assistant asked for a meeting with the boss to explain what was happening and to show the results of the log. After the situation was fully explained, highlighting everyone's frustrations, and when the appropriate hourly rates were included in this calculation, it is easy to see the outcome.

The initial decision made by the boss was to leave her Personal Assistant alone to complete the important work and while that was being done she would get her own coffee from the cafe. The Personal Assistant had a better idea: it was suggested that the boss change her taste in coffee, or even just stop drinking so much coffee—or better still, put a coffee machine in the boss's office!

The boss laughed, and finally agreed to the last suggestion. The Personal Assistant was asked to go downstairs and buy a coffee machine for the boss. Seconds after that request was made it was withdrawn. The boss then said, 'You continue on with your important work, and I'll go downstairs and buy the machine myself'!

The first column in this sample time log is used to record every event, project, activity, interruption and so on that you get involved with during the day. Every time you move on to something different, the new activity must be noted. A partially completed sample log is shown below for your reference.

Sample time log

Activity	Time	Priority	Comments
Read morning paper	20	C	Should do before work
Do report to CK	20	A	Always do A's first
Phoned Chris	5	B	Make calls before lunch
Phoned Lee	10	C	Do during lunch break
Meeting with Sam	40	C	Have in their office

The time log

Activity	Time	Priority	Comments

The second column is used for the time duration—how long it took you to do. This is recorded in minutes, not in hours. If you find that you're putting entries down with time-frames of 2–3 hours, that may not be correct. By far the majority of people cannot remain involved in one activity for that length of time. There will be many interruptions during that time, all of which need to be recorded as separate entries. Question every entry that is more than 20 minutes in duration.

The third column is used to put down the priority level of the activity. Use the priority levels A, B, C, and D. (You will see what they are shortly.) Be prepared for a bit of a shock when you complete your time logs, because when you finish the 2-week period you will need to sit down and analyse the information you have. It's pointless having the information if you don't process it!

The fourth column is used for general comments. While you are writing your entries and they are fresh in your mind, put down your ideas. That way, if something has worked well for you, you can use it again. If something hasn't worked so well, you can write down some ideas for doing it better next time.

We will refer back to this time log later.

You may prefer to use another type of time log, where you set up a grid to work with. This has the advantage that you can see quickly where your time is going in the different types of activities. The disadvantage is that it may take a while to identify the different categories you will need in the time log. You may need to run the log for a trial period to get it right.

Below is a sample of a completed grid time log.

Time Log				Day					
Meetings Formal	**Meetings Informal**	**Phone calls**	**Coffee**	**Filing**	**Reading**	**Training**	**Repairing things**	**Travel**	**Writing**
20	5	5	10	10	10	30	10	20	10
25	10	10	5	15	10	20	20	30	15
20	15	5	10		15		5		20
45		5					10		
		10							
110	30	35	25	25	35	50	45	50	45

Here's a blank one that you may like to copy for your own use. Select your own categories to work with.

Grid time Log　　　　Day _____

_____

_____
_____
_____
_____
_____
_____
_____
_____
_____
_____
_____
_____
_____
_____
_____
_____
_____
_____
_____
_____
_____
_____
_____
_____

Your typical day

Think about your typical day. How much of your time would you normally spend working on really high-priority items? Tick the appropriate box below, and be honest. This estimate is for your whole waking day, not just time you spend in the workplace!

Time typically spent on high-priority activities

10%	
20%	
30%	
40%	
50%	
60%	
70%	
80%	
90%	
100%	

If you're being totally honest with yourself, you will probably have ticked somewhere around the 20 per cent area. It's found that most people only spend around 20 per cent of their time working on the really high-priority items, while around 80 per cent of the time is spent working on the low-priority ones.

This falls into the Pareto principle. Most people have heard of Vilfredo Pareto, who was an Italian sociologist. Way back in 1895 he hypothesised that 80 per cent of the value is in 20 per cent of the time spent.

What we need to do is to identify what makes up the current 20 per cent so that we can start to expand on it. And the only way to expand on it is to start reducing on the 80 per cent of low-priority items.

The 80:20 rule applies to just about everything, not only to time management:

- 80 per cent of the time you go out for dinner will be spent at 20 per cent of the restaurants you normally go to.
- 20 per cent of your carpet will get 80 per cent of the wear.
- 80 per cent of your interruptions will come from 20 per cent of the people you deal with.
- 80 per cent of your sales will come from 20 per cent of your clients.

Let's expand that point a little further. As just mentioned earlier, a salesperson will probably find that 80 per cent of their sales come from 20 per cent of their customers. If they identify this 20 per cent of customers and focus their time on them, increased sales should follow. They may also find that the bottom 20 per cent are actually costing them money. It's the Pareto principle again.

The Pareto principle is **always** right—at least 80 per cent of the time!

Sometimes people don't realise when they are involved in low-priority items. Every time we pick up something different to do we must ask ourselves, 'Why am I doing this?' or 'Why do I need to do this?' If you can come up with a valid reason for doing or completing this activity, continue on. If you can't come up with a valid reason, then you have a couple of options to think about.

If you don't know why you're doing a particular activity, at least put your hand up and start asking some questions of the people around you. If these people can't give you a valid reason for doing it, then drop it! Don't waste your time doing low-priority items or items of low value.

Your time log will identify some of the low-priority items that can be modified, delegated or dropped completely.

Setting priorities

NOTES

Before we can set priorities we need to develop a list to be prioritised. Yes, it's the old 'to do' list. However, the term 'to do' list is outdated. It should be called a 'prioritised daily action list'. That's a far more positive term. It's a list of things that need to be done on a daily basis—a 'PDAL' or simply a 'daily action list', or 'action list'.

This list will act as a constant reminder during the day of the things that still need to be done. If the list isn't in front of you during the day it will be forgotten and things will not get done. One of the most important qualities people look for in others these days is dependability. These lists will help develop that skill.

Your list should be thorough, but not finish up the size of your local telephone book. Don't try to take on too many things. If you do, you're only setting yourself up for failure. And if you keep failing, what will happen to your motivation after a while? The list needs to be specific and achievable. This makes it motivating.

Story has it that when Charles M. Schwab was president of Bethlehem Steel, he confronted I. V. Lee, a management consultant, with an unusual challenge. 'Show me a way to get more things done,' he demanded. 'If it works, I'll pay anything within reason.'

Lee handed Schwab a piece of paper. 'Write down the things you have to do tomorrow,' he said. Schwab did it. 'Now, number these items in the order of their real importance,' Lee continued. Schwab did that. 'The first thing tomorrow morning,' Lee added, 'start working on number one and stay with it until it is completed. Next, take number two, and don't go any further until it is completed. Then proceed to number three, and so on. If you can't complete everything on schedule, don't worry. At least you will have taken care of the most important things before getting distracted by items of lesser importance. The secret is to do this daily. Evaluate the relative importance of the things you have to get done, establish priorities, record your plan of action, and stick to it.

'Do this every day. After you have convinced yourself of the value of this system, have your other staff try it. Test it as long as you like, and then send me a cheque for whatever you think the idea is worth.'

In a few weeks, Charles Schwab sent I. V. Lee a cheque for $25 000. Schwab later said that this was the most profitable idea he had ever learned in his business career.

This is an impressive story. But when you realise that this took place many decades ago, you can see that the $25 000 idea was worth an enormous amount of money to Charles Schwab.

Unfortunately, most people's 'to do' list or 'action list' is far too long. It needs to be kept to a reasonable number of items. The questions listed below will assist in keeping your list to a reasonable size.

Questions for preparing a manageable daily action list:

- Of my long-range and intermediate high-priority goals, which should I work on today?
- What will help me reach these long-range and intermediate high-priority goals today?
- Which projects will give me the highest return on my investment?
- Is there a deadline to work to?
- Which project will be the greatest threat to my survival if I don't do it?
- Which project will be the greatest threat to my company if I don't do it?
- What projects does the boss want me to do?
- What wasn't completed yesterday that needs to be done today?
- What do my personal values suggest I should be doing?
- What does company policy suggest I should be doing?
- Is there anything else that may yield long-term results?
- What will happen if I don't do it?

However, a list by itself is not enough, as we shall see.

You sit down in the morning, get your pen and paper out, and write your list of things that need to be done today. You finish writing the list and look at the size of it. You have listed 100 items that you would like to complete today.

You start working through the list by looking at it and asking yourself which item you will do first. Perhaps the telephone calls get done first; perhaps the mail gets sorted next; maybe the filing gets done after that. You finally get to the end of the day. You look at your list again and see that you have ticked off ninety-seven of the hundred original items and you congratulate yourself on the completion of so many tasks. You then notice that the three things that haven't been ticked off were the three most important items on the list!

You see that today wasn't as productive as you had originally thought. You can now start to rationalise. Today wasn't as productive as it should have been, but at least now you can say you've ticked off the ninety-seven little things so that tomorrow you

can just focus on the other three really important things. But what comes in overnight? Another ninety-seven trivial things that need to be done!

To avoid this situation we need to set realistic priorities on this list and work to these priorities as the day goes along. But, very importantly, we need to have some flexibility built in so that the extra things that come up during the day can also be dealt with.

We now need to prioritise this list by asking some more questions.

Questions to help prioritise the daily action list:

- What will give the greatest long-term results?
- Which item will give the highest payoff?
- On a long-term basis which items will make me feel best to accomplish?
- Will it help me reach my potential?
- Does it require other people to assist me?
- Is it a directive from someone I can't ignore?
- Which projects does the boss consider most vital?
- Is it important to someone I really care about?
- Will it really matter a year from now?
- What will happen if I don't do it at all?

You may have noticed that none of these questions asks us to prioritise using urgency as a criterion.

Urgent versus important

NOTES

Some people seem to think that 'urgent' and 'important' mean the same thing. Nothing can be further from the truth. There is a huge difference between them.

To demonstrate the difference, I have shown below a 4-quadrant matrix. This matrix identifies the four categories into which tasks, projects or activities can fall.

What happens if an event or an activity is:*	Vital or important?	Not vital or not important?
Urgent?	(Quadrant 1)	(Quadrant 3)
Not urgent?	(Quadrant 2)	(Quadrant 4)

* In each box, write 'gets done' or 'doesn't get done' according to human tendency.

Quadrant 1

If we have a task that falls into quadrant 1 (the top left-hand quadrant), that means it is both vital and urgent. So does it get done? Yes it does. But why does it get done—because it's vital, or because it's urgent?

These jobs usually get done because of their urgency.

What projects do you complete that fall into quadrant 1?

_____

_____

_____

_____

Quadrant 2

If we have a task that falls into quadrant 2 (the bottom left-hand quadrant), that means it is vital but not urgent. When does it get done? Usually these jobs get done when they become urgent.

Quadrant 2 is the most important of the four quadrants. This is the one we need to keep in mind all the time. It will identify the activities that are really important to us, and it will also allow us to work on them before they really do become urgent. If we wait for these things to become truly urgent, the quality of our decisions will generally suffer.

At the end of this chapter there are two questions for you to spend some time with. These questions will prompt you into thinking more about quadrant 2 activities.

What projects do you complete that fall into quadrant 2?

_____

_____

_____

_____

Quadrant 3

If we have a task that falls into quadrant 3 (the top right-hand quadrant), that means it's not vital but it is urgent. Do these tasks usually get done? Yes they do. But when we look more closely at these tasks we can see that not all of them have to be done.

Most people tend to react to a sense of urgency. A simple request lands on your desk, you pick it up and look at it, you take the necessary action and then you pass it on. There was a perceived sense of urgency, but probably no importance (or very little) attached to this task.

Some things in quadrant 3 do have to be done, but some things don't. You're sure to find that there are a number of things you're currently doing that fall into quadrant 3 and which don't have to be done. Stop doing these things. Instead, give yourself some more time to work towards the things that can make a tremendous positive difference for you, both personally and professionally.

> **What projects do you complete that fall into quadrant 3?**
>
> _____
>
> _____
>
> _____
>
> _____

Quadrant 4

If we have a task that falls into quadrant 4 (the bottom right-hand quadrant), that means it's not vital and it's not urgent. Do these jobs usually get done? Unfortunately, yes, these jobs sometimes do get done. Why? Because they tend to provide a change of pace, or they may be good fill-in jobs, or maybe they fit into the spare 5 minutes we have available to us before the next coffee break.

If you ever find yourself doing any quadrant 4 tasks, stop doing them straight-away. They are usually a complete waste of your time and effort. Stop doing these things, as well as the unnecessary quadrant 3 activities identified previously. As I said before, give yourself some more time to work towards the things that can make a tremendous positive difference for you, both personally and professionally.

> **What projects do you complete that fall into quadrant 4?**
>
> _____
>
> _____
>
> _____
>
> _____
>
> _____

The chart gives some examples of activities that fall into the four quadrants.

The four quadrants

	Vital or important?	Not vital or not important?
Urgent?	Quadrant 1: • **Immediately productive activities** • **Problems to do with our responsibilities** • **Deadlines to be met**	Quadrant 3: • **Some interruptions** • **Some meetings** • **Some reports**
Not urgent?	Quadrant 2: • **Planning and preparation** • **New opportunities** • **Relationships**	Quadrant 4: • **Trivia** • **Most time-wasters** • **Some of the pleasant activities**

Questions for you to improve your focus

What are five things you're **not** doing now that, if you did on a regular basis, would make a tremendous positive difference for you at work?

1. _____

2. _____

3. _____

4. _____

5. _____

What are five things you're **not** doing now that, if you did on a regular basis, would make a tremendous positive difference in your personal life?

1. _____

_____

2. _____

_____

3. _____

_____

4. _____

_____

5. _____

_____

Now select the most important activity from each of the above boxes. So which one thing, if you did it on a regular basis, would make a tremendous positive difference for you at work, and which one thing would make a tremendous positive difference for you in your personal life? Mark both of these with the letter 'A'. Mark all the others with the letter 'B'.

Now that you have marked all the items that could make the most difference for you both professionally and personally, turn to page 165 and write yourself another two goals.

- Your first goal will be to develop an action plan to start working on the two items marked 'A' within 7 days of writing this goal—or perhaps after reading through this book—but don't take too long!
- Your second goal will be to develop an action plan to start working on the other items, marked 'B', within 28 days of starting the others. Please put the appropriate dates beside these two goals.

Go the extra kilometre—it's never crowded!

We need to ask ourselves constantly whether the activity we are involved in, or about to be involved in, is getting us closer to the goals that are important to us.

What's really important to us?

NOTES

It is easy for most people to develop a list of things that need to be done, but it's only the successful people who have the ability to focus on the really important items.

Previously I showed you how to develop a 'daily action list', but I didn't explain fully how to set priorities on the items. This section will show you how to set realistic priorities on these tasks. It should be looked at together with the ten questions for prioritising a daily action list on page 54.

After your list of things to be done (daily action list) is completed you need to ask yourself a series of questions. First you need to ask, 'What is vital on this list? What is vital to me, to my position or to my organisation today?' The dictionary definition of vital is 'life sustaining'. We aren't talking about life-sustaining activities, but the things that are super-important to us.

When you have identified the vital activities, mark them with the letter 'A' to indicate their vital importance.

Then read through the remainder of the list and ask yourself, 'What else is important, but not as important as the 'A's?'. When you can identify what else is important to yourself, or your position or your organisation, then mark those items with the letter 'B'. This indicates that the task is important, but not as important as the 'A's; 'B's should therefore not be done at the expense of the 'A's.

The 'A's and 'B's will generally take up about 20 per cent of your list to start with.

Read through the remainder of your list and ask yourself, 'What else, if I did it today, would have some value for me?'. Once you can identify the items that would have limited value for you, mark those with the letter 'C'.

If you go through your list now and see that there is anything on it that isn't marked A, B or C, those items should be marked with the letter 'D'. A 'D' indicates that it would be a complete waste of time to do it. 'D' stands for dump it or delete it, not for delegate it! 'D's are a complete waste of time for everyone. It's even a complete waste of time writing these things down. You will find that after a while you won't even bother writing the 'D's' down.

After the priorities have been set on your list, start working through the list, beginning with the highest priority. If for any reason that activity can't be started or completed, simply go on to the next-highest priority. If you use this type of approach you will find that you are working on your highest priorities constantly during the day.

A = vital

B = important

C = some value

D = don't do it!

You should expect the odd urgency or crisis to present itself. As they do, handle them as efficiently as possible so that afterwards you can immediately go back to your high-priority activities.

As we saw earlier, most people do respond to a sense of urgency, so we can now turn that around in a positive way for ourselves.

If we place an asterisk beside something on a list, what does it do? It makes it stand out, or highlights it. It creates a sense of urgency. So another symbol we could use on a prioritised list would be the asterisk. It can be used by itself on an item, or it can be used in conjunction with a letter priority. But don't make it too complex. If you make it too complex you will look at the list in the morning and say to yourself that you will get back to it later. And you know as well as I do that you won't get back to it. People are basically lazy. Always look for the easy way of doing things.

A = vital

B = important

C = some value

D = don't do it!

* = urgent

It's a fact that your conscious mind can effectively focus on only one thing at a time. By identifying tasks or goals and setting realistic priorities, then working through your list as described, you will ensure you are focusing on the correct activities. You will see some techniques further on in this book for dealing with these situations.

Unfortunately most people don't focus on their vital priorities. By identifying the important activities and setting realistic priorities you will be able to start focusing on your most vital priorities.

Just a quick reminder of something that was said much earlier. Anyone can show you how to do it, but it's up to you to actually go and do it!

While we're talking about doing things, how about putting a few more ideas on pages 177–84.

What do we need in front of us?

It is simple! The things that we need in front of us are the things that are really important to us. These are the things that we need to work on before they become urgent.

These things need to be accessible to us, because if they're not accessible to us now, they will get forgotten. And we don't want to forget about the important things, do we?

The things that we need in front of us include our lists of things that need to be done, the meetings we have to attend, the appointments we may have, the reports that need to be written, stock lists, inventories and so on.

The item we use to make all of these things accessible is a personal organiser.

Using diaries, organisers or other planning tools

NOTES

Have you ever put something away in a safe place and never been able to find it again?

Don't try to remember everything. Write it down. But don't rely on notes scribbled on scrap pieces of paper, or on those little sticky notes, or notes on the front of your refrigerator, or notes on the back of business cards. If you have information scattered all over the place some things will inevitably be overlooked. I can see from the grin on your face that you may currently be doing some of these things!

All of these notes need to be in one central and accessible location. That is what a 'personal organiser' is used for. Regardless of what it's called—personal organiser, organiser, planner, scheduler—they should all mean the same thing. It's a place where we can enter and retrieve notes, information, facts, figures, data or other information, without anything being overlooked. But it needs to be used properly.

The diary is no longer just seen as a simple appointment book. It's a key tool used in planning and organising. With a properly structured system you will need to refer to only one source for all of your appointments, notes, addresses, lists of things to do, goals, projects and so on.

There are many varied systems available these days. Look through them all to find the one that suits you best. The one I personally recommend (and obviously use myself) is the Day-Timer junior desk model, using a 2-page-per-day format. This is the one shown in this book for the application examples. These ideas can also be used on other systems; it's just a matter of adapting the ideas to suit.

Shown below is a suggested format for creating a personal organiser. It is only a suggestion and should be treated as such. For a system to work correctly you must first identify what you would like to achieve using a personal organiser, and then build the system around those requirements.

My system

My personal organiser, as an example, has a leather zip binder to keep everything together and safe. Inside it has a full year schedule sheet (to see the whole year at a glance). Then I have my address and phone directory. That is followed by my current month's monthly calendar, followed by this month's pages. Then I have

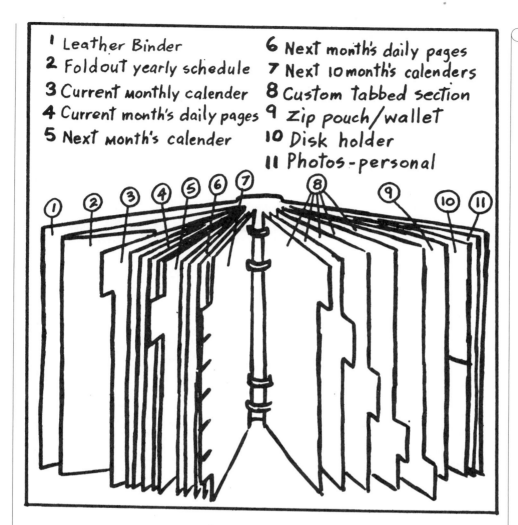

1 Leather Binder
2 Foldout yearly schedule
3 Current monthly calender
4 Current month's daily pages
5 Next month's calender
6 Next month's daily pages
7 Next 10 month's calenders
8 Custom tabbed section
9 Zip pouch/wallet
10 Disk holder
11 Photos-personal

next month's monthly calendar, followed by its daily pages. Then I have the rest of my monthly calendars for the next twelve months.

After that comes the true custom section. I have a number of tabbed dividers set up for different things. To give you an example, some of the tabs are marked 'Personal life goals', 'Goals with the company', 'Incubation ideas', 'Personal information', 'Books', 'New house', 'Accounts' and so on. You will have to think about the categories you would use.

At the back I have a zip pouch that I use as a wallet (cash, driver's licence etc.), along with a couple of plastic credit card holders.

As you can see, the system I use is very comprehensive. And it works!

Creating your own system

Once you have built a system don't assume that it's going to work perfectly to start with. Be prepared to make some mistakes, but make sure you learn by these mistakes. Admit them, and then improve on them! Perhaps even the things that do work well can be improved.

The monthly calendar

We will start by looking at the use of the 'monthly calendar'. This is used for time-related and date-related activities. It gives you an overview of the month or the week at a glance. The choice is yours on how you use it. It can be used to show entries such as meetings to attend, appointments you have planned, deadlines, important dates, social activities and any other activity you would like to include.

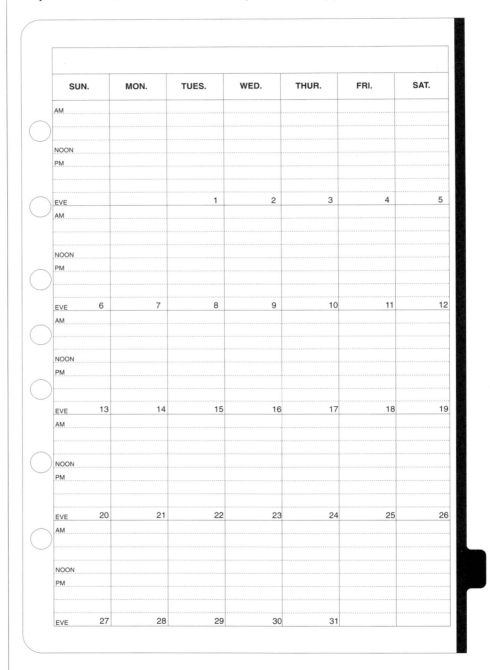

	SUN.	MON.	TUES.	WED.	THUR.	FRI.	SAT.
AM							
NOON							
PM							
EVE			1	2	3	4	5
AM							
NOON							
PM							
EVE	6	7	8	9	10	11	12
AM							
NOON							
PM							
EVE	13	14	15	16	17	18	19
AM							
NOON							
PM							
EVE	20	21	22	23	24	25	26
AM							
NOON							
PM							
EVE	27	28	29	30	31		

By including all the different activities you get involved in, you can now use the monthly calendar as a balancing tool if you need to. By showing them all, you can make sure you include all the things that should be covered over this period of time.

For example, if you looked at your monthly calendar and saw that everything on it was a business activity, it would remind you that you probably have other responsibilities outside the workplace. On the other hand, if you looked at your monthly calendar and saw that everything noted was a social activity, the message would be not to forget that you probably have responsibilities in the workplace as well!

The daily boxes on the monthly calendar aren't very big, so you need to be very concise with the information. This actually makes it more effective. I suggest you limit the information on the monthly calendar to a time, the name of a person or a meeting, and a place if necessary.

Let's look at a few examples. Assume that you have an 8.00 am staff meeting every Friday morning. This would be noted as follows.

	SUN.	MON.	TUES.	WED.	THUR.	FRI.	SAT.
AM						8 STF.MTG	
NOON							
PM							
EVE			1	2	3	4	5
AM						8 STF.MTG	
NOON							
PM							
EVE	6	7	8	9	10	11	12
AM						8 STF.MTG	
NOON							
PM							
EVE	13	14	15	16	17	18	19
AM						8 STF.MTG	
NOON							
PM							
EVE	20	21	22	23	24	25	26
AM							
NOON							
PM							
EVE	27	28	29	30	31		

You will see that there is no location shown for these meetings. Because you are entering the information yourself, you can safely make certain assumptions. Your assumption would be that the meeting is going to be held in its normal location. If the meeting was to be held away from its normal location, then, and only then, would the location be shown.

Now assume you're talking to someone—let's say Lee—about a particular project, and Lee wants to continue this conversation or meeting with you next month.

What you do now is look forward to your calendar for next month to see when you would be free to continue this meeting.

Let's assume that the last diagram is your monthly calendar for next month. You will see that the whole month is still pretty much free. You then let Lee know the whole month is open and ask what dates would suit. Lee might suggest that Friday the 4th would be good, so you can now look specifically at Friday the 4th. You can see that you have a staff meeting at 8.00 am and you know that will go for about an hour. You can then say to Lee that any time after 9.00 am would suit you. Lee suggests 10.00 am. You now enter these meeting details on the monthly calendar. This is shown below.

	SUN.	MON.	TUES.	WED.	THUR.	FRI.	SAT.
AM						8 STF.MTG	
						10 LEE(13/7)	
NOON							
PM							
EVE		1	2	3	4	5	
AM						8 STF.MTG	
NOON							
PM							
EVE	6	7	8	9	10	11	12
AM						8 STF.MTG	
NOON							
PM							
EVE	13	14	15	16	17	18	19
AM						8 STF.MTG	
NOON							
PM							
EVE	20	21	22	23	24	25	26
AM							
NOON							
PM							
EVE	27	28	29	30	31		

You will notice that next to the entry with Lee there is a set of brackets or parentheses. These are the most powerful referencing system you can use. They simply tell you where to refer to. By putting today's date inside these brackets it's easy to find the information regarding that meeting, because while you're talking with Lee you take all of the notes regarding this meeting on today's page. So now you can find the details when you need them.

Remember the definition of planning shown earlier? Planning is to identify future events and bring them into the present so that we can do something about them now.

So before you go to the meeting with Lee you need to refer back to the pages that show the details of the meeting. In this case it's 13 July. You can then transfer information if you need to, or take it with you.

Why don't we put the information directly onto the meeting date page while we're talking with Lee? Because if we do that it may mean carrying around a year's worth of future date pages with us, and that's not terribly practical. By transferring the information, either on the morning of the meeting or perhaps the day before, it also means that the information or points will be fresh in your mind. So there will be even less chance of overlooking anything.

At 8.00 pm on the first Friday in every month you have to attend an association meeting. That would be shown as follows.

	SUN.	MON.	TUES.	WED.	THUR.	FRI.	SAT.
AM						8 STF.MTG	
						10 LEE(13/7)	
NOON							
PM							
						8 ASS.MTG	
EVE			1	2	3	4	5
AM						8 STF.MTG	
NOON							
PM							
EVE	6	7	8	9	10	11	12
AM						8 STF.MTG	
NOON							
PM							
EVE	13	14	15	16	17	18	19
AM						8 STF.MTG	
NOON							
PM							
EVE	20	21	22	23	24	25	26
AM							
NOON							
PM							
EVE	27	28	29	30	31		

You can see that the entries are being placed in the correct time sequence. The top of the box is the beginning of the day, and the bottom of the box is the end of the day. If things are put in out of sequence it can create confusion. And if confusion is introduced, stress levels will increase and productivity will fall.

The next question to ask ourselves is, 'What should we use to write with on the monthly calendars—a pen, a pencil, or perhaps both?'

Several time-management experts told me many years ago to use only a pencil in any kind of diary system. And when you think about it, it makes a lot of sense. So I used a pencil exclusively for a number of years. But what eventually happened was that, flicking back through old pages trying to find previous information, I found that a lot of the earlier entries had worn off the page, probably from the pages rubbing against each other, or simply from constant flicking through the pages.

So what I suggest to people now is that they use both a pen and a pencil. A pen is used for entries that will not change, and a pencil for entries that are subject to change. That way, if they are changed, it's simply a matter of getting out the eraser and moving the entry to the new location. This saves crossing things out and creating confusion.

If a pencil entry is confirmed, or goes ahead as planned, the entry should be gone over with a pen. This will ensure the information is permanently recorded so it can be retrieved later if necessary.

When selecting a pen and pencil for your organiser look for ones with very fine tips. That way, if you write three or four words in the box it won't fill it up in one go. If you have a large handwriting style or if your handwriting is messy, you should find that a fine-tip pen or pencil will also assist in overcoming these problems.

Other examples of entries you may see on a monthly calendar could include the following.

	SUN.	MON.	TUES.	WED.	THUR.	FRI.	SAT.
AM						8 STF.MTG	
			TP	TP	930 RPMTG		
NOON			ADEL.	ADEL.		10 LEE(13/7)	
PM							2 F/BALL
		615 AN105		5 AN144			630 J&J
						8 ASS.MTG	
EVE		1	2	3		4	5
AM						8 STF.MTG	
		INTERVIEWS		TP	11 BRIAN L		
NOON				SYD			
PM	2 ROD						
					7 RAY M		7 P&L
EVE	6	7	8	9	10	11	12
AM						8 STF.MTG	
NOON							
PM	BBQ						2 F/BALL
EVE	13	14	15	16	17	18	19
AM				9 BRIAN L		8 STF.MTG	
	DIVING	11 MDMTG	TP		10 BM(2/4)	BRIS	
NOON			SYD				
PM						5 AN153	
					650 AN142		8 MOVIES
EVE	20	21	22	23	24	25	26
AM				CBR			
NOON			12 DAVE H				
PM			6 AN5973	6 AN5974			
		8 EL MICH					
EVE	27	28	29	30	31		

You will see that vertical lines can be used to block off large periods of time. If the example shown above was your monthly calendar and someone wanted to see you on Monday the 7th you would be able to say to them that you could be available in the afternoon, because you can see that you are tied up all morning in interviews.

Let's say that part of your monthly plan is to spend four days per month out of the office visiting your clients. You will see how these four days have now been blocked off to keep the days free for these external appointments, that is from the 14th to the 17th. If you need to, you can also superimpose these external appointments directly over the top of these days that have been blocked off.

Colours and highlighters can also be used to draw attention to important dates and deadlines. The colours make them stand out so that you will notice them well in advance and do any relevant pre-work.

Not all of the dates can be highlighted, of course, so use the colour highlighting technique only for the really important dates and deadlines.

Regular dates and activities must be included. List the regular activities you get involved with so that they don't get double-booked or overlooked.

Have you ever done anything on a very regular basis and then one day made a commitment with someone else to be at a different place at the same time?

Can you truthfully say that you've never forgotten anything? By writing these things down there is far less chance of forgetting them. There's an old Chinese proverb that says, 'The palest ink is better than the best memory'. It's really true. Simply by writing these things down you have far less chance of forgetting them.

The daily activity pages

The monthly calendar lets you see the month or the week at a glance. It gives you an overview of that period of time. It lets you see the broader picture, without giving the details. The detailed information is shown on the 'daily activity pages'.

The daily activity pages should be formulated to give you details of information needed during the day. By far the most popular format used is the 2-page-per-day system as shown above. This format has a number of benefits. It shows you the appointments and meetings that have been set. It shows you what needs to be done during the day. It allows you to write in advance reminders when needed. It lets you record your expenses for tax purposes or reimbursement. And it allows you to record information during the day.

Appointments and scheduled events

Let's start by looking at the 'appointments and scheduled events' section on the left-hand page. This section is used to note appointments and meetings that have been scheduled for the day. It looks at the non-discretionary time you have during the day—non-discretionary in that you no longer have control over this time. You have previously made a commitment to be somewhere at a certain place with a person, or a group of people.

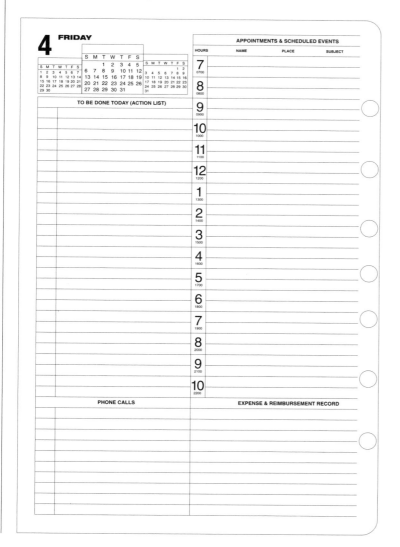

To use the 'appointment and scheduled events' section properly, what you should do each morning is to look at your monthly calendar. This will give you a general overview. Then you should look at today's box, and copy across any meetings or other activities that have been noted for today. Yes, it is a duplication of information, but there's a valid reason for doing it.

If you look at your monthly calendar each morning and copy across any items you have noted for the day, that means that they will be fresh in your mind, and that reduces the possibility of forgetting them.

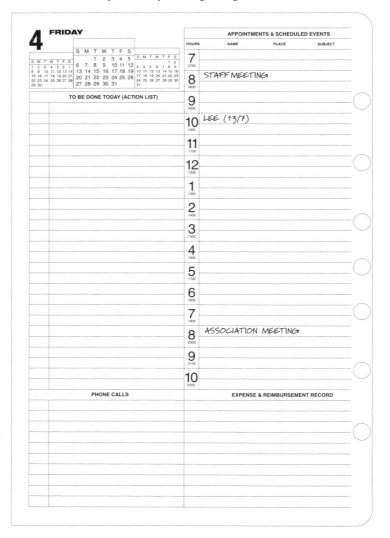

Let's look at the examples shown above on the monthly calendar for Friday the 4th. On the morning of the 4th we would copy over the staff meeting, the appointment with Lee and the Association meeting.

If you use your organiser correctly and it's sitting on your desk in front of you during the day, or on the car seat beside you, and you're scanning over it regularly looking at appointments you've written down in the morning, what are the chances of not turning up for one of those meetings? The percentage chance has to be pretty close to zero!

Do you find that you never seem to have time to work towards your long-range or important goals? Here's an idea that might work for you. Think about the possibility of making an appointment with yourself occasionally. That way if someone wants to see you during the day you can now say that you are unable to see them during certain times because of previous commitments.

Alternatively, rather than make an appointment with yourself, maybe you could make an appointment with a particular project. That way you can close your door between certain times and work on the really important items. If you need to find time to work towards your important goals and projects, this is one idea that may work for you. Give it a go and see what happens.

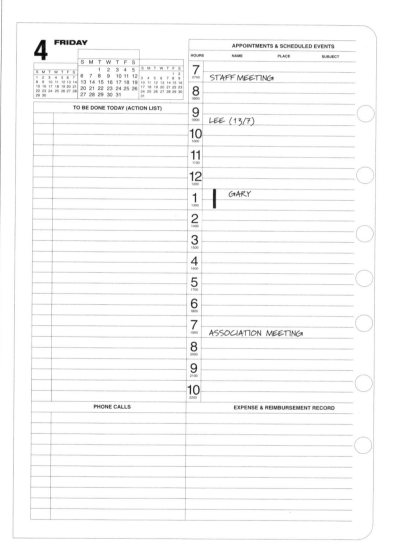

The daily action list

Going to the left of the page, the next box is the 'action list'. This is the list of things that need to be done during the day, often referred to as the 'to do' list. The action list looks at the things we can do during our discretionary time— things that haven't been allocated particular time slots during the day. There are always certain things that we would like to do during the day, but we aren't locked into certain times to do them. You can shuffle these things around and work on them when you want to.

Everyone has different amounts of discretionary time. Some people only have 10 or 15 minutes' worth of discretionary time during the day, whereas others may have 10 or 15 hours' worth. Your time log should identify approximately how much discretionary time you have during the day.

The action list should be broken into two separate parts. This is an important part of maintaining balance. The top part of the list could be used for work-related activities, while the bottom part of the list could be used for personal tasks and activities. By breaking it into two separate parts you are covering both parts of your life, both in the workplace and outside the workplace. If you look at the list and there isn't at least one entry in the top part and one in the bottom part, you could be missing half of what it's all about. So come back and look at that area again.

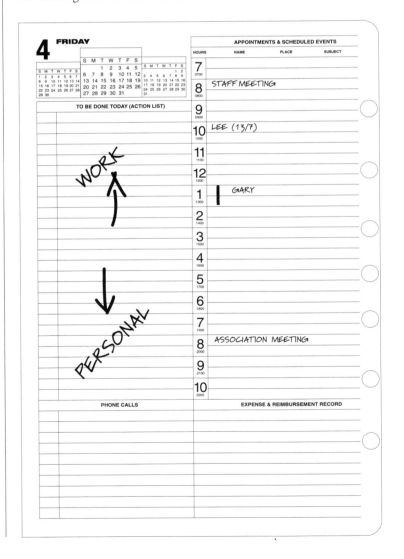

Before you write anything at all on your action list, you need to ask yourself twelve questions. We have looked at these questions previously (in the chapter 'Setting priorities'). These questions will help keep the list to a reasonable size. Unfortunately, most people include far too many things on their action lists, and if we don't complete the list regularly our motivation can fall dramatically. Your list should be comprehensive, but it shouldn't be as thick as an encyclopaedia.

Here are the twelve 'questions for preparing a manageable daily action list' again:

- Of my long-range and intermediate high-priority goals, which should I work on today?
- What will help me reach these long-range and intermediate high-priority goals today?
- Which projects will give me the highest return on my investment?
- Is there a deadline to work to?
- Which project will be the greatest threat to my survival if I don't do it?
- Which project will be the greatest threat to my company if I don't do it?
- What projects does the boss want me to do?
- What wasn't completed yesterday that needs to be done today?
- What do my personal values suggest I should be doing?
- What does company policy suggest I should be doing?
- Is there anything else that may yield long-term results?
- What will happen if I don't do it?

Asking these twelve questions will help you to keep the action list to a reasonable size which can be handled effectively during the day.

Once you have asked yourself these questions, you can start to put some entries on the action list. You can see from the example shown below that there are eight things that need to be done at work today, and four things that need to be done outside the workplace.

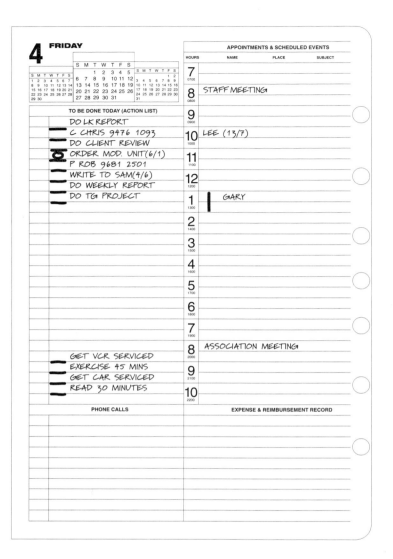

Going through the two lists, you will see the first entry for work today is to do the LK report. You will notice that there has been an indentation created to the left-hand side of all of the entries. This indentation is creating a second column. Two columns are required with any type of action list (whether printed or imagined). You will see why as we work through this example.

The second entry is to call Chris. You will see I've started to introduce abbreviations. The 'C' means call, a 'P' could mean phone, an 'F' could mean fax, 'W' for write, 'S' for send, and so on. Most people write words longhand all the time. Think about using codes and abbreviations where appropriate. Cut down on some of the writing time if you can; it all adds up. It also gives you more room on your page and it doesn't look so cluttered. This will help to reduce stress levels.

The next entry is to do the client review. This is followed by the ordering of the modular unit. You will see this also has a date reference beside it. This shows that all the information regarding the modular unit is located back on that page, should it be required for any reason. You will also notice a circle in front of this entry. We will come back to this shortly.

The next entry is to phone Rob; there is a phone number shown with it. The next is to write to Sam, with a date reference. Then do the weekly report, followed by the completion of the TG project.

These are all the things that need to be done at work today.

One thing that isn't obvious is that none of these items on the work list is more than 20 minutes in duration. If you had a report to do, and you estimated it would take 2 hours to do, when would it get done? It would probably be done 2 hours before it was due. Why do we keep putting it off? Because it will take 2 hours, and we keep waiting for a free block of 2 hours to do it! How often do people get free blocks of 2 hours? Very rarely.

Current research suggests that the average person is interrupted every 5–20 minutes in the workplace. Commonsense therefore suggests that we should plan jobs of no more than 20 minutes in duration. That 2-hour report should therefore be broken into at least six separate pieces.

So how do we break it down? Maybe we need to get a copy of last month's report; maybe we need to get another four separate files out; maybe we need to speak to three other people about this report. The 2-hour report has now been broken into at least eight separate jobs. So the first three can be done today, the next two tomorrow and the final three could be done the day after.

Break larger jobs into chunks so that they can be digested one at a time.

How do you eat an elephant?
One bite at a time!

Current research also suggests that most people can plan for only 40 per cent of their paid work day. That means that 60 per cent of the time the average person is paid to 'put out bushfires'.

I'm sure you've done it in the past. You did the right thing in the morning. You got out your sheet of paper and pen and listed things to be done during the day. When you finished the list you looked at it and thought to yourself, 'Maybe there's too much to do on this list'. So you then decided to put some time-frames against each job. 'How long will each of these take me to do?' The first job had 10 minutes marked beside it, the next job had 30 minutes, the next 15 minutes, the next 1 hour, and so on.

You then totalled the allocated times. Fifty-seven hours! 'I can't get 57 hours' worth of work done today, so what can I take off the list?' You finally got the list down to 8 hours. You're reasonably happy now. You're ready to start working on the list and the phone rings. You're now behind 5 minutes for the day. You won't achieve everything on the list. What happens to your motivation after a while? It goes down fairly quickly, and after a while it becomes non-existent!

Don't set yourself up for failure. Allow time for the unplanned interruptions and the bushfires to occur. They will happen, there's no question about it, so allow time to deal with them. Don't overcommit yourself.

And remember—the more time you spend with customers or clients, the more time you should allow to put out the bushfires.

In the lower section of the list you will see are four things you would like to do for yourself: get the video cassette recorder serviced, exercise for 45 minutes, get the car serviced, and read for 30 minutes.

Now that you have these two lists developed, the next thing you need to do is to prioritise all the items.

Prioritising the action list

Let's start with the workplace.

What you need to do now is ask yourself, 'Which of these items are vital to me today at work?'. What is vital to your position or to your organisation? Once these items are identified they should be marked with an 'A'. Remember earlier, when we looked at setting priorities?

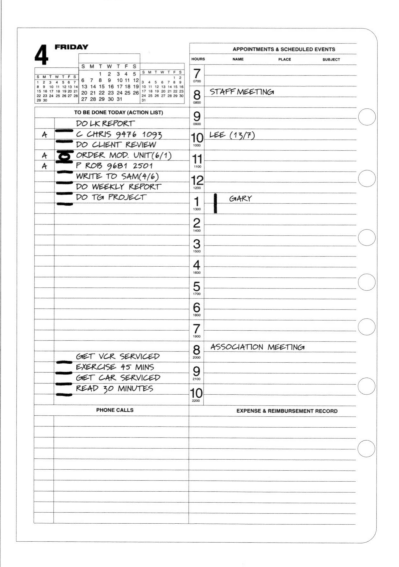

You can see three items are marked as vital. It's vital today that you call Chris, order the modular unit, and phone Rob.

Moving down to the next priority level you now need to ask yourself, 'What else is important, but not as important as the A's? These items are marked with the letter 'B'.

4 FRIDAY

S M T W T F S
1 2 3 4 5 6 7
8 9 10 11 12 13 14
15 16 17 18 19 20 21
22 23 24 25 26 27 28
29 30

S M T W T F S
1 2 3 4 5
6 7 8 9 10 11 12
13 14 15 16 17 18 19
20 21 22 23 24 25 26
27 28 29 30 31

S M T W T F S
1 2
3 4 5 6 7 8 9
10 11 12 13 14 15 16
17 18 19 20 21 22 23
24 25 26 27 28 29 30
31

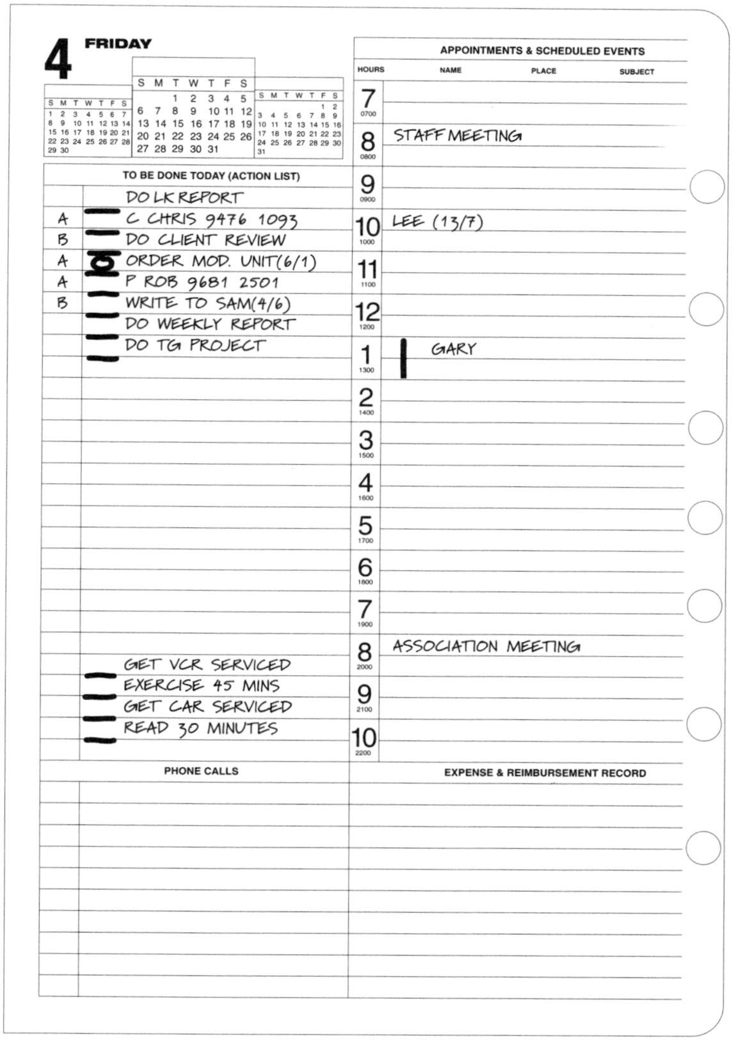

TO BE DONE TODAY (ACTION LIST)

	DO LK REPORT
A	C CHRIS 9476 1093
B	DO CLIENT REVIEW
A	ORDER MOD. UNIT(6/1)
A	P ROB 9681 2501
B	WRITE TO SAM(4/6)
	DO WEEKLY REPORT
	DO TG PROJECT
	GET VCR SERVICED
	EXERCISE 45 MINS
	GET CAR SERVICED
	READ 30 MINUTES

APPOINTMENTS & SCHEDULED EVENTS

HOURS	NAME / PLACE / SUBJECT
7 (0700)	
8 (0800)	STAFF MEETING
9 (0900)	
10 (1000)	LEE (13/7)
11 (1100)	
12 (1200)	
1 (1300)	GARY
2 (1400)	
3 (1500)	
4 (1600)	
5 (1700)	
6 (1800)	
7 (1900)	
8 (2000)	ASSOCIATION MEETING
9 (2100)	
10 (2200)	

PHONE CALLS

EXPENSE & REIMBURSEMENT RECORD

Now on to the third level: 'What else would have some value in being done today?' These items are marked with the letter 'C'. That's to do the LK report, do the weekly report and to do the TG project.

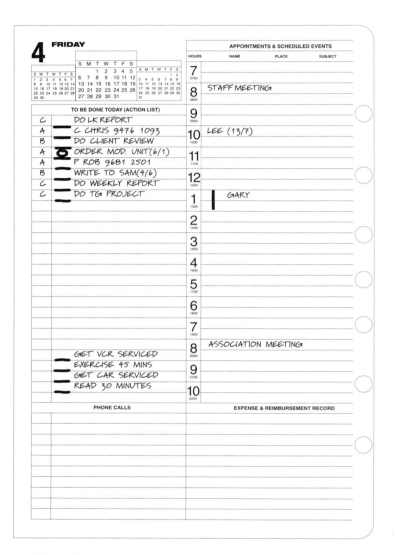

You will very rarely use the letter 'D'. As we said before, it's a complete waste of time writing these things down at all.

We can now apply the same process to the bottom part of the list, except there is now an asterisk beside getting the car serviced. This is taken a little further than I suggested before. The asterisk tells you that it has to be done today, and there's no way out of it.

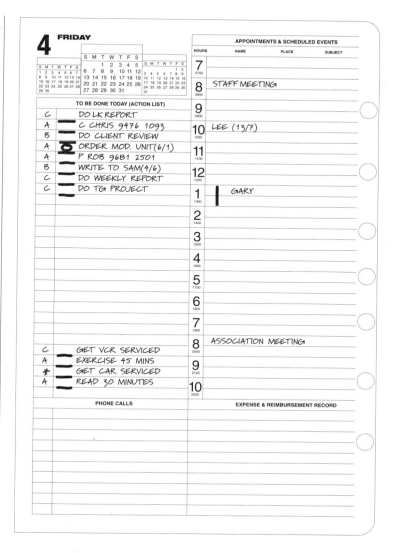

Exercising and reading both link in with a couple of your long-range goals, so they are both marked with the letter A. There would be some value in getting the video cassette recorder serviced today, so that gets marked with a C.

Everything now has a letter code beside it. So in the workplace today, which job should you start working on? Most people will say that you should start working on the A's. That's right, but is it a fantastic use of your time to work on three jobs at the same time? You do have three jobs marked with the letter A, after all. No, it's not a good idea!

So which A should you start working on? The one at the top of the list? The most urgent of them? The quickest one? The one that will take the most time to complete? The ones that involve other people? The phone calls because they're quick and easy? The one the boss wants first? The one with the circle in front of it because it looks different? The ones that are time-framed? The easiest one of them? The hardest one?

That's eleven selection criteria so far. The problem is, they're all wrong! What you need to do is to prioritise the priorities based on order of importance. So ask yourself, 'Which is the most important A?', not which is the quickest, or the easiest, or the most urgent, and so on.

Looking at your three A priorities, you know that calling Rob is far more important than ordering the modular unit, and that's more important than calling Chris. So mark these A1, A2 and A3, showing their order of importance.

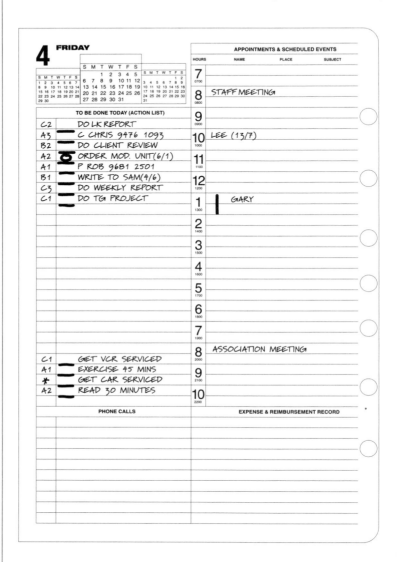

The same process applies with the B's. Writing to Sam is more important than doing the client review. So that determines your B1 and B2.

Similarly, with the Cs: doing the weekly report is more important than the LK report, and that's more important than the TG project. So you have the C1, C2 and C3, again based on order of importance.

The same process applies to the bottom section of the list. Exercising is more important than reading, so you can decide the A1 and the A2. There's only one C, so that's got to be the C1.

Let's have another look at the 'questions to help prioritise the daily action list':

- What will give the greatest long-term results?
- Which item will give the highest payoff?
- On a long-term basis which items will make me feel best to accomplish?
- Will it help me reach my potential?
- Does it require other people to assist me?
- Is it a directive from someone I can't ignore?
- Which projects does the boss consider most vital?
- Is it important to someone I really care about?
- Will it really matter a year from now?
- What will happen if I don't do it at all?

We now have a fully prioritised list, and it should take only a few seconds to do this. Don't spend 35 minutes trying to work out which should be the C27 and the C28. Just pick a number in this case and get it out of the way (the prioritisation, that is, not the task!).

Putting priorities into practice

Let's get back to the workplace today. Which job should you now start working on? Some people might say that you should get the car serviced first, but it's on the wrong list! This is where we need some flexibility built in. Getting the car serviced normally has to be done during business hours. So if you didn't drop the car off on the way into work, you would probably make a phone call as soon as you get to work to get this underway.

So let's say the car has been taken care of. Which A should you start working on now? Obviously the A1—the phone call to Rob.

If it's so obvious, why do people usually start working on the Cs? Because they're easier to do! It may be a fair change in focus to turn up for work and start working on the high priorities. However, they're much easier to do if you break them into smaller pieces to start with.

But back into the real world. Rob doesn't turn up for work until 11.00 am most days. So what do you do now? It's commonsense to go on to the A2. But commonsense would also say that when we finish the A2 we go on to the A3, not back to the A1. So how do you make sure you don't forget the phone call to Rob at 11.00 am?

You could put an asterisk beside it. That will work, but it means then that you have to review every action. You could reprioritise it, but that would mean going back into third-generation time-management skills, not the fifth level we are now looking at. The marking A1 tells us that it's the most important thing that needs to be done today, but it may not be necessarily the first thing that you can work on.

What you should do is to place the phone call to Rob over at 11.00 am in the 'appointments and scheduled events' section of the page. What you have done now is made an appointment with yourself to make the phone call at 11.00 am. By doing that, and making sure that you scan over the pages regularly during the day, it means that at 11.00 am you will pick up the phone and call Rob.

Some people might ask why you can't just call Rob's office and leave a message for him to call back? How often do people return your phone calls? Every time? I doubt it. You need to control the vital jobs.

The A1 has been taken care of, so what now? On to the A2—ordering the modular unit. So now you can call someone into your office to do it for you. Why? Because when you planned your day, you said that someone else could do it for you. That's what the circle in front indicates. The circle says, delegate.

After the job has been delegated, I suggest you then put the person's initial inside the circle. That shows you that the job has been taken care of, and who is responsible for it.

If you delegate work to lots of people, and need to keep track of all the delegations, you could set up a tab section inside your organiser for the sole use of delegations. You could have a separate page for everyone you delegate to. Their name would be shown at the top of the page, and when you give them something to do you could note on their page, when you gave it to them, what the task was, and the follow-up date.

By using that kind of technique you could use the 'delegations' pages as part of your initial planning for the day. All you need to do is scan through the pages to see if there's anything outstanding. If there is, simple transfer a note over to today's page to speak with that person and find out what happened with the job you gave them to do.

The A2 is taken care of, so let's move on to the A3—the phone call to Chris. This could be one of those unusual jobs where it gets ticked off! There will be some days when you get only one thing ticked off your list, but as long as it's an A that's okay. Always go for quality rather than quantity.

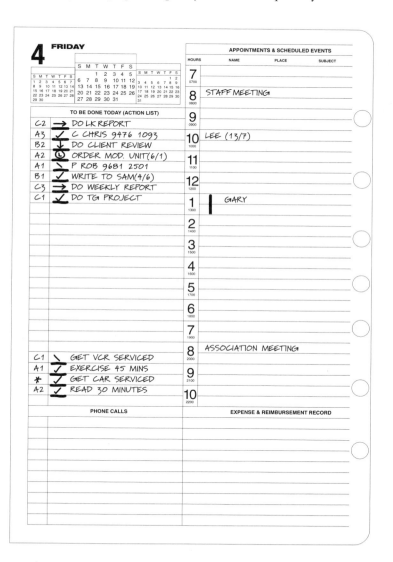

Now that the A's are taken care of, you can start on the B's. The B1 was to write to Sam. That's been done, so it gets ticked off. The B2 is to do the client review. You make a phone call to the person who initially requested it to be done. They tell you it hasn't got to be done now. So a down arrow could be placed against this entry. The down arrow indicates that the task or activity has been dropped or deleted.

On to the C's. The TG project is done, so tick it off. It's now 5.00 in the afternoon—time to finish work, but there are two items left on the list. However, they are the C2 and the C3. Isn't it better to have the C2 and the C3 sitting there untouched, rather than the A1 and the A2?

The C2 and the C3 can be done tomorrow, so they get carried over the page. The two original entries on today's page get marked with a right arrow. The right arrow indicates that the task or activity has been carried forward further into the system.

One other point here is that we cannot pre-prioritise jobs. What's an A today could be a D tomorrow; and what's a C today could be an A tomorrow. All we do is to put the entries forward so that they won't be forgotten or overlooked. They will be prioritised on the day itself, not before.

That's the top half of the list, now we can go down to the lower section, our personal items.

Getting the car serviced was certainly done, so that gets ticked off. Exercising and reading were done, so they get ticked off. Getting the VCR serviced wasn't done, but it has a partial tick beside it. That may show that a phone call was made, but there are things to be done. This partial tick system ensures that nothing gets overlooked or forgotten at the end of the day.

Reviewing the day

At the end of the day you need to have a review. Go through the lists and, if there's anything left over, it now needs to be applied to the 'rule of the four Ds': you can Do it, Defer it, Delegate it, or Delete it. There are no other choices; that's it.

Rule of the four Ds

Do it
Defer it
Delegate it
Delete it

You also need to check that all the items marked with a partial tick have been completed, or further action is noted to follow up. By doing this, you won't overlook anything.

The bad news is that, no matter how good you are with your plan at the beginning of the day, someone is bound to come along and dump something else on you.

As these additional items come in, don't just add them to your list and reprioritise everything. Just note them in between the other two lists. They don't require priorities set on them. Then, as you finish one job on your original list, and before you go on to the next priority, just ask yourself: 'What's the most important use of my time right now?' That will help you out of any reactive situation.

More functions of the daily activity page

The two boxes at the bottom of the page can be used for phone calls and expenses. If you need to make lots of phone calls during the day they can all be placed together here. As we should try and do like tasks at the same time that will assist here. And also try and work out the best time of day to do some of these things. Outgoing phone calls are generally best made around 11.30 am to 12.00 noon, and 4:00 to 5:00 in the afternoon. That tends to be the time when most people are in their office. That will save time trying to catch them.

The expense and reimbursement box can be used for tax purposes or for the reimbursement of expenses. If you don't need it for these reasons, use it for something else. You could use it as a shopping list, for keeping track of your squash scores, for football results, whatever suits you. Just because the words are shown there doesn't lock you in for that sole application.

Look over to the right-hand side of the two-page format. The right-hand page can be used for diary entries or as a work record. Any notes you need to record during the day should be shown here. It can be used to keep track of notes, conversations, quotations and so on. It can also be used to keep track of your time during the day for charge-out purposes, if you charge your time against specific jobs.

If you do need to keep track of your time during the day for charge-out or billing purposes, then you have an application for the blank time column shown on this format. You can also get formats with a column at the left-hand side of the page to show times during the day. You should now be able to see that when you link that column in with the other blank time column you can start to keep track of where your time has gone during the day.

If you don't need to keep track of your time for billing reasons, then I suggest you completely ignore the times shown at the side of the page, if you have any there. I suggest this because these times will usually lock you in to 15 minutes per line, and that's not the way you should use the larger column in the centre of the page.

As mentioned previously, this column (the diary and work record) should be used to keep track of important conversations that have taken place during the day, along with notes of verbal quotations given or received. It could also be used as a personal-type diary with a written script of notes that you would like to record. It can be used for any notes that you may normally take on scrap pieces of paper. The major advantage of using this page instead is that you will be able to find your notes again later when you need them!

There are three sample entries shown below. The first shows the telephone conversation with Rob Beavis. While Rob is coming to the telephone, or while the initial socialising is taking place, Rob's name and telephone number are being written at the top of the page. Rob's name is then underlined, in case the information is needed later on. Then, when this page is referred to later, rather than having to read through the whole page trying to find the entry, you will need only to scan through the underlined or key words.

DIARY AND WORK RECORD			FRIDAY 4		
REF.	NAME OF PROJECT		DETAILS OF MEETINGS - AGREEMENTS - DECISIONS	TIME HRS.	1/10
1	<u>ROB BEAVIS</u>		9476 1093		
2	●	1.	MTG. ON 15TH		
3		2.	MTG. AT 2PM		
4		3.	MTG. AT ROBS		
5		4.	ROBS ADDRESS		
6			....		
7		5.	DIRECTIONS		
8			....		
9	●	6.	P JOHN		
10	●	7.	P CHRIS		
11					
12	<u>AWARDS PRESENTATION</u>				
13			AN AWARDS PRESENTATION WAS		
14			HELD AT RICHMOND WHERE SAM &		
15			MICK WERE PRESENTED WITH		
16			....		
17					
18	<u>JOHNS VCR REPAIR SHOP</u>		9457 2200		
19		1.	SPOKE TO JOHN		
20		2.	QUOTE TO FIX $175—		
21		3.	NEW VCR $450—		
22		4.	IF IN TOMORROW—READY BY NEXT		
23			FRIDAY		
24					
25					
26					
27					
28					
29					
30					
31					
32					
33					
34					
35					
36					
37					
38					
39					
40					

As the conversation proceeds, any important points get noted underneath. These entries are indented from the left and numbered. The first entry shows that another meeting has been arranged for the 15th of next month. The second entry shows that the meeting will be at two o'clock in the afternoon. The third entry indicates that the meeting will be held at Rob's office. Some people prefer to put down just one entry rather than these three separate entries. This may be written as '2 o'clock meeting on 15th at Rob's'. There's no right or wrong way of doing this; it's just a matter of personal preference.

Notice that three of the entries have bullet points shown to the left-hand side of them (entry numbers 1, 6 and 7). This indicates that there are three outstanding things to do as the result of this telephone call with Rob.

As soon as the call has ended you should now ask yourself the question, 'What's the most important use of my time right now?'

As you can see, you now have three areas to select tasks from: the original prioritised daily action list, the second list that was created during the day in the centre of the prioritised daily action list, and the entries on the work record page with bullet points beside them. Let's assume that in this case you decide that you are going to carry out the three entries that resulted from the call with Rob.

The first entry is probably just a matter of going to next month's monthly calendar and noting the appointment for the 15th. The second entry involves a telephone call to John to see if he can make the meeting on the 15th, so you make that call. After the call has been made to John, someone comes into the office and the telephone call to Chris gets overlooked (sound familiar?).

Now you can see how important it is to have a review of this page at the end of the day (one review at the very least). By carrying out this review you will realise that you have forgotten to make the call to Chris. So again you need to apply the rule of the four Ds: Do it, Defer it, Delegate it, or Delete it. These are the four choices you have with any outstanding entry. In this case you know that Chris has gone home at this time of the day, so you defer it as an action that needs to be carried out tomorrow.

The telephone call to Chris is then shown as an advance reminder on tomorrow's action list. Remember that these advance reminders cannot be pre-prioritised. They are prioritised on the day, because priorities can change over time.

You can see that having a review at the end of the day avoids a situation where things can get overlooked or forgotten.

The next sample item gives an example of a personal-type diary entry. It's just a script of things that may have happened during the day. I know of one person (a politician) who went through all of their previous diary entries over a number of years and is using that as the basis of a novel.

The last entry is the phone call that was made to get the video cassette recorder fixed. The telephone call was made to John's VCR Repair Shop. The first entry says, 'Spoke to John'. Sounds very simple, but how many times have you rung a service provider and been told that they will call you back tomorrow and let you know about something. You wait for the call and it never comes. You then have to ring the company back again. You don't know who you spoke to, so you have to explain the whole story again to someone else. If that's happened to you in the past, then you can see a valid reason for noting your contact person.

John in this case was a very cluey person, who knew exactly what the problem was. He said to fix it would cost $175. He also said that they had some very good deals going on new VCRs right now, and that a new one could be purchased for $450 rather than having the old one repaired. He said that if the repair was to be done, things were fairly quiet in their service area right now, and that if the VCR needing repair was taken in tomorrow it would be ready by next Friday.

Another big advantage here is the possibility of being able to prove contemporaneous notes at a later date (from the Latin, meaning: belonging to the same time, existing or occurring at the same time, of the same age or date, of the present time). Just imagine, one of your previous clients from years back comes to you and claims that information that you gave them several years ago was incorrect and that as a result they're going to take legal action against you for damages. Wouldn't it be great to be able to go back to your old diary notes and show what was actually said on that day?

You could find that, from a legal point of view, these notes will be worth their weight in gold should any dispute arise at a later date. Check with your legal adviser if you need more specific detail on this.

If you fill the 'diary and work record' completely before the end of the day, you should have some way of including extra pages in your system. DON'T use scrap pieces of paper. As soon as you do, you'll start losing information.

It's a good idea to have some additional pages, referred to as 'add-in pages' at the back of your system. That way, if the pages fill up before the end of the day, you can open up the binder and insert the necessary pages. These additional pages won't get lost and the notes on them can be found later as they have now been properly date referenced.

But how do we find this information again later when we need it? We need an information retrieval system.

Retrieving diary information

I think you will agree with me that it's pointless writing things down if you can't find them again later on. There are many ways of retrieving information. What we will do now is look at the four most popular ways of doing it.

Brackets

You have already seen the first way, which is to use brackets or parentheses. These tell you to refer to whatever is contained inside them. The couple of examples you have seen so far had only date references inside them. Use your imagination! Perhaps it's also possible to put other things inside them. Perhaps you could refer to a personnel file or a client file. Perhaps you could reference to a page in a book or a computer disk or a computer file name. The only limit here is your creativity. If you need to go anywhere to find something, put it straight inside the brackets so that you can find it again instantly and accurately. Don't put it off. You know as well as I do that if you put it off for too long it will take hours to find again later. Remember the question at the beginning of last chapter? Have you ever put anything away in a safe place and never been able to find it again later? Don't put it off, do it now!

Your old monthly calendars

The second way of finding things is to use your old monthly calendars. For example, suppose you need to find some information from an important meeting you attended about this time last year. What you could do is to get your monthly calendars out from last year and look at the one for the equivalent month last year, along with the month before and the month after.

What you are doing is looking through those three pieces of paper trying to find the meeting note. Once you find that, you can open up to the correct daily activity page for the specific details. This means that you are looking through three pieces of paper rather than something like ninety-two pages of information.

This example also shows you that, if sometime during the day you need to attend a meeting that wasn't planned for in the morning, you need to make a note of that meeting on the monthly calendar. This calendar could become the index for all the daily activity pages behind it.

Flagging the page

Another way of retrieving information is with the use of paperclips or 'Post-It'® notes.

Imagine that you have just made a diary note on today's page. You know that you will need the information again later, but you don't know when you will need it. All you need to do in this case is to flag the page with a paperclip or a 'Post-It'® note. It may be worthwhile to show a key word on the 'Post-It'® note as well. At the end of the month all the daily pages are taken out for the month and filed away.

These pages can be put away in a box or a ring binder. When I reorder my yearly pages I have them supplied with a storage case. This a ring binder for all of the year's pages plus any additional notes.

A couple of months down the track you need the information. All you have to do now is go through your storage sets looking at each of the pages that have been flagged. Yes, you could still be looking through quite a lot of paperwork, but it's certainly better than looking through every piece of paper!

This method works best if no more than six or seven flags are used each month. It's guaranteed not to work if you try to use thirty-one flags each month—you can't make everything stand out.

The card index

The other popular way of retrieving information is with the use of a carding system. Index cards are easy to obtain. They are generally about 15 by 10 centimetres, with lines printed across them, and are normally a light-weight board or very heavy paper.

Perhaps you have a series of meetings with a particular person regarding a specific project. All your diary entries should be entered by date reference on the index card for that particular person. This means that every person and organisation you deal with regularly should have their own card. Set the cards up alphabetically so that it is relatively easy to find them as required. If you prefer using a computer, these records can be kept on an appropriate database; the same principles apply. The Day-Timer Organiser software is good for this.

At the end of the month you will need to go through all your diary entries and, for each diary entry that relates to a specific person, project or organisation, enter the information on the relevant card. Not all the information needs to be shown—only the date reference and key words are necessary.

Customising your organiser

Your organiser should also have the facility to keep other information handy for retrieval when needed. What most organised people do is to include a special tabbed section in their organiser for this purpose. That way, everything you need is stored in one central location.

The tab headings might include:

- personal life goals
- unassigned action list
- business projects
- reading lists
- client notes
- stock lists
- business goals
- travel details
- hobbies
- special ideas
- phone numbers, and so on.

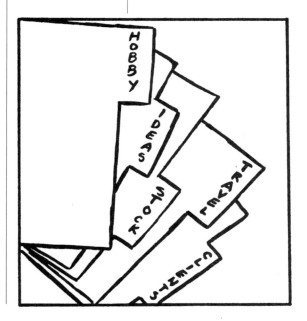

You may want to include special headings relating to particular projects or meetings. You may have a tab set up to keep track of the projects you give to other people to look after. You may like to set up a special tabbed section for all of your personal details or financial records. It's up to you!

The more creative you are, and the more imagination you have, the better off you'll be using the tabbed section in your organiser. If you think you're lacking in the area of imagination or creativity, ask someone else for help or suggestions.

Computerised systems

There are some very powerful time-management software packages available but the one major disadvantage with them is that they may not be visually accessible for most of the time. While the screen is out of sight the lists of things to be done, the meetings we have, and so on, are generally out of mind. The computer should therefore be seen as a supplementary part of the paper-based personal organiser. The computer should be seen as a communication device, especially on a networked system using electronic calendars.

For example, let's assume you work with ten other people and you would like to arrange a meeting with them. What you should be able to do is use the network to search through everybody's electronic calendar to identify a common time that they all have available for this meeting. You should then be able to book that time with them through the network so that when they come back into their office they will find a message on the screen to tell them that the appointment has been made with you.

Additionally when each person comes back into their office they should enter any appointments they have made while out of the office. Electronic calendars, like any other kind, must be kept up to date or they won't stand the slightest chance of working effectively. It takes only one person to let the whole system down. Any computerised system should also have a requirement for the receiver to either 'accept' or 'reject' any appointment that has been made without their direct knowledge. That way you won't have unexpected appointments popping up and catching you unawares.

The computerised system may also be used as an additional tool to support a paper system. Sales people, for example, can use it to track detailed conversations, orders or inquiries with customers. It can also be used for project management tasks.

If it's going to be used for any of these purposes, make sure the software can print to the correct size paper—that is, the size of paper you are using in your personal organiser. Again, Day-Timers have a range of specifically designed software packages that can meet these requirements. These also have the advantage of being able to print to prepunched pages that will fit all their systems. Day-Timers can supply the blank prepunched pages.

If you are considering the use of an electronic system, it must be integrated with a paper system. They have to work together.

Make life easy for yourself

Before selecting any computerised system, however, make sure you check out the manual paper systems available. You may find that a simple carding system with follow-up diary notes may be the most effective way for you.

Use the 'KISS' technique:

**Keep
It
Simple
Stupid!**

Too many people make things confusing for themselves. If you make it too complicated you won't do it. If you create a complicated system, you will find yourself picking it up in the morning and saying to yourself, 'It's too hard now, I'll do it later'. And you know as well as I do that you probably won't pick it up again. Keep it simple, because we are all basically lazy! Always go for the easy way of doing things. If you want a good system designed, give it to the laziest person you know to do.

Some more ideas

You may also like to consider using a whiteboard, a magnetic board or similar for a group 'action list'. That way everyone can see how their tasks fall into the bigger picture. Any relevant activity is then taken from the bigger picture and duplicated into their individual personal organisers.

The popular 'Post-It'® notes can be used the same way. Simply break projects into smaller tasks, put each task on a single 'Post-It'® note, stick them on a piece of paper, or on a whiteboard, or on the side of a refrigerator, or on the front of a filing cabinet, or other prominent place, then rearrange them into a suitable sequence. The advantage of this is that you can rearrange things without having to start everything again.

'Post-It'® notes have many applications from an organisational point of view. Just don't use them by themselves as your total personal diary system!

If you find that you need to take lots of notes during the day, think about using an engineer's handbook for taking the notes. An engineer's handbook is the same as most other spiral-bound books, except that it has prenumbered pages. The prenumbered pages allow you to find information instantly. You can find it instantly because you should have a built-in referencing system.

To illustrate this let's look at an example. Let's assume that you had a meeting with Lee at 9.30 am. The basic meeting information would be shown on your daily pages as '9.30 Lee'.

Let's now say that you had taken the notes for this meeting in your engineer's handbook. Your diary note would now read something like this: '9.30 Lee (v 3 pp 23–27)'. This shows you that all the notes taken for this meeting are located in volume 3 of your handbooks and specifically referenced to pages 23–27 of this handbook. Obviously you would also have a date reference on the relevant pages in your handbook so that you could refer to the dated pages in your organiser later if necessary.

What you have just looked at is the starting point for your own customised personal organiser. You now have to sit down and decide what you need to do in regard to setting up your own system. DON'T rely on your memory to keep track of everything; you already know that things will get overlooked.

As stated earlier, there are few qualities more important in business or social situations than dependability. If you don't have a constant reminder of things you would like to get done, they won't be done.

Even with a plan in place, always keep asking yourself, 'Is this the most important use of my time right now?' If it's not, then ask, 'What is?'

Always ask yourself:
'Is this the most important use of my time right now?'
If it's not, then ask, 'What is?'

Keep your plan with you all the time. Make it accessible. This is most easily done by putting all the important items together as one single system. Using a personal organiser effectively allows you to unclutter your mind and focus on just one thing at a time.

When selecting or creating a system, make sure it's simple to use. A complex system has the disadvantage of being time-consuming for the user. If you would like to purchase a Day-Timer system like mine (the one shown in all of the above examples), you will find an order form located at the back of this book (page 197). Simply copy the order form, fill in the relevant details, and post it off. DON'T wait—that's procrastination, one of our biggest time-management problems!

If you fail to plan,
then you plan to fail.

What would I look for in a personal organiser?

What are some of the tabbed sections I could include in my personal organiser? What would be really handy for me?

_____

_____

_____

_____

_____

_____

_____

_____

_____

_____

_____

Now that you have listed the items you would look for in a personal organiser, turn to page 165 and write yourself another goal. Your goal will be to order or obtain this organiser within 24 hours of writing this goal. Please put the appropriate time and date beside this goal.

Things should be made as simple as possible.
Albert Einstein

Typical time-waster 1:
The office environment

NOTES

We really do have to put things away some time or other. So why not try to put things away as we go? This will make it much easier to find them again next time we need to use them.

An additional benefit here is that we start to look more professional. How often do you see very successful people sitting in the middle of clutter? Not often, I suggest. In fact I've never seen one in a cluttered environment. All the successful people I've ever spoken to have had an amazingly clean and tidy desk.

Make the workplace a more efficient and comfortable place to work in. You spend an enormous amount of time in your work area, so why not make it work better for you? Even consider the type of furniture you have. If you feel more comfortable in your chair, your performance should be enhanced.

Attack your desktop!

If you currently have a messy desk you must invest some time in sorting it out. We are using the example of a desk, but the same principles apply to any work area, whether it be a desk, work bench, work station, factory area, outside shed or motor vehicle. The techniques also apply to the 'electronic office'.

Start by taking EVERYTHING off your desk. While everything is off, it's a good idea to get out a cloth and some furniture polish. It's probably been years since it was cleaned properly!

Then you need to put all the paperwork, reports and projects that were sitting on your desk in one large pile. Break the larger stack into four smaller stacks: an 'A' stack, a 'B' stack, a 'C' stack, and a 'D' stack. Yes, it's the same as setting priorities. These four piles stay on your desk until everything has been prioritised.

The A stack includes all the vital tasks and activities—all the vital reports, projects and paperwork.

The B stack includes all the important tasks and activities that are important, but not as important as the items in the A stack.

The C stack holds the items you consider to be unimportant. There could be some value in working on these projects and reports, but they are very limited in their value.

The D stack is made up of things that are a complete waste of time—both yours and other people's. This stack is immediately placed in the recycling bin. Thanks to Mr Pareto (mentioned earlier) 20 per cent of your paperwork has just been thrown away.

You now need to pick up your B stack. The B's are no longer allowed to be B's. They have to be re-sorted as either A's or C's. Again using the Pareto principle, you will find that 20 per cent of your B stack has now become priority A and the other 80 per cent has become priority C. That will leave you with two piles of paper, an A pile and a C pile.

Now pick up your A stack. These items need to be prioritised further. You need to identify the most important items, which you mark A1. Then select the second most important A and mark it A2, and so on.

When all the A's have been prioritised and the tasks have been entered in your organiser, the A stack should be placed in one of the drawers at the side of the desk, or in the filing cabinet immediately beside or behind you.

The A stack should not be placed on the desk in front of you. If you do this, you will finish up at the end of the day with the A's scattered all over your desk. If they are left in your line of sight, you will be subconsciously working on them during the day. The key point here is to keep the A stack accessible to you, but not visually accessible.

That leaves the C stack. You need to look around your office and find a filing cabinet with a couple of empty drawers. This is where the C stack goes. Open up one of the drawers, put the C's in it and then forget about them. Yes, that's right, close the drawer and forget about them.

You're probably sitting back thinking to yourself that some of those C's might turn into A's. I agree with you, they probably will. But a C priority will not turn into an A priority overnight without some kind of warning. You will get a follow-up memo, a follow-up phone call, or someone knocking on your door asking about it. When you get the follow-up request, you then go over to the C drawer and flick through the stack until you find the piece of paper you need. You then take this piece of paper out of the drawer, close the drawer, and prioritise the C piece of paper in with the other A's.

Some people have suggested that we should set up a filing system for the C priorities so that we can find them when we need them. But why should we set up a filing system to find low-priority items? Sometimes it's better to 'bite the bullet' and accept the fact that it may take us 1 or 2 minutes going through the C pile trying to find the piece of paper we need. This is by far a better use of our time than setting up an elaborate filing system, and spending more time maintaining it, just to find the low-priority items.

After a few days, weeks or months, you will find that the C drawers are bursting at the seams. You then need to take all that paperwork out of the drawers and re-sort it. The Pareto principle now comes back into play. As you go through these items you will find that 80 per cent of them will be thrown in the bin.

The other 20 per cent will probably be thrown away next time you sort them.

All you are doing is giving the C's an ageing period. After a while they will die a natural death. If any need to be revived before then, you know exactly where to go to find them.

That then takes care of all of the paperwork on your desk. It sounds like a huge project, and it is. After you've cleaned up, you need to become a little more reactive to the paperwork as it comes in. Yes, that's right—reactive to the paperwork as it comes in—but only reactive to the prioritisation, not to the doing of it. It's automatically classified as A or C, or it goes in the bin. If you don't maintain the system it will take only a few days to get back into the rut you were in beforehand.

What now?

Your desk is now completely bare! What are some of the things you will put back on it after you've cleaned up? (Please remember that these ideas apply to all situations, not just to an office desk.)

Now use your imagination. You've just invested a great deal of your time getting rid of everything from your desk. You're looking at a completely blank slab of timber. Absolutely nothing at all is on your desk. After you've cleaned up, what are some of the things that you're going to put back on your desktop? After all, you can't have a completely clean desktop, can you?

The items you may consider putting back on your desktop could include items such as:

- your personal organiser
- the basic working tools you need to work with
- your telephone
- a computer
- personal items
- in-trays
- the project you are currently supposed to be working on.

Let's look at these items to see how necessary they are.

Personal organiser

Your organiser should be sitting on your desk, open at today's date, so that you can see what needs to be done today and what appointments and meetings you have.

Working tools

Your basic working tools need to be located on top of your desk. If you use your pen, pencil, hole punch, calculator, ruler and stapler regularly during the day, that's where they need to be located. You shouldn't have the whole stationery cabinet on top of the desk, just the basic working tools that you use regularly during the work day.

Telephone

Most people would suggest that the telephone needs to be located on top of your desk. By far the majority of people have their telephone sitting right at the very front of their desk, right in front of them. This may or may not be appropriate. If you have your telephone sitting in front of you, what is it saying to you during the day? 'Use me', is generally what it's saying. And sometimes you just keep doing what it's asking you to do, even though it may not be an appropriate action for you to perform.

If you can say that a telephone is not an essential part of your job, then perhaps it might be worthwhile moving the telephone to the side of your desk. That way it's out of sight and the visual distraction you had sitting in front of you is no longer a possible time-waster. If you do need to spend the bulk of your time on the telephone during the day, leave it in front of you, because it's something you need to focus on.

Computer

Most people these days work with computers. I thought that people had stopped playing with computers, but I have been proved wrong on many occasions. By just observing some people and talking with others, it's easy to see that many people could be wasting up to 80 per cent of their time with their computers.

Imagine this. A person gets a request in the mail. They go to their computer and start to key in their reply. After the information has been entered they run their spell check, their grammar check, and every other check they have on the system. They then do a draft read of the document on the screen and notice a few changes that need to be made to their original document, so they make these changes as they read through.

After the changes have been made they run all of the checks again. They then decide to print the document, so they push the print button on the keyboard. Then they stand up and walk over to the printer to get the copy.

While they are walking back to their desk they scan through the document and notice a couple of other changes that need to be made. They go back to the keyboard and make these changes. They push the print button again, go back over to the printer and pick up the second copy of this letter.

Again, while they are walking back to their desk, they notice a few more changes that need to be made. So they go back to the keyboard and make the changes. This time they think they'd better run all the checks again. They press the print button on the keyboard. They get the third draft copy to read through, then the fourth, then the fifth, then the sixth, then the seventh. Seven copies of the letter have been generated!

Here's a question for you to think about. Is it essential for ALL of your paperwork to be absolutely perfect? Yes I agree that some, if not most of it, needs to be perfect. But think about this situation as an example. You are sending out an internal office memo about the staff Christmas party for this year. Does it really matter if the graphic for the Christmas tree is only 5 cm high rather than 5.2 cm high? It's not going to make any difference, so let it go through!

Much earlier in the book, we mentioned 'futzing'. Futzing is spending three hours changing the background colours of your computer screen and selecting a nice background graphic. You're busy on your computer perhaps, but busy doing the wrong things! Are YOU guilty of futzing?

If you don't need to spend the bulk of your day working on your computer, or if you spend too much time playing with it, then think about moving it so that it's sitting beside you or behind you. Move it so that you don't continually keep responding to it or to the games that may be loaded on it, because you can see it all the time. You may be setting yourself up in reactive mode.

If you do need to spend the bulk of your day working with your computer, then the best spot for it is on your desk right in front of you. In this case it needs to be in front of you, because it's a tool you need to focus on during the day.

Personal items

You will probably put back some of your personal items on the desk—your coffee cup or tea cup, a vase of flowers, photographs of your favourite people or possessions. When you put them back, however, just make sure they are not likely to distract you.

I had a person on a seminar once who said he had a photograph of his partner on his desk, but he had to take it off. He said he found it too much of a distraction. Someone else in the audience asked how long he had been married. He responded by saying that he had been married for around 9 months. The other person in the audience told him to leave it there because: 'Things will change!'

The in-tray

Lots of people have an in-tray on the desk. If you have one on your desk, ask yourself this question. Do you need to respond to the pieces of paper that are placed in it immediately they are received?

Some people don't realise how much time they lose during the day because of interruptions. Who creates most of our interruptions? We do! Most people don't realise that they cause most of their interruptions themselves.

If someone puts a piece of paper in your in-tray, what do you automatically do? You pick it up and have a quick

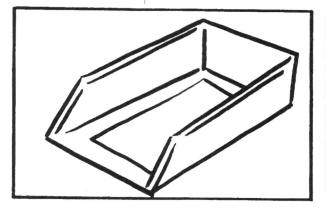

look at it. What do you do with it then? You put it back in your own in-tray. One very basic rule with an in-tray is the fact that you never put anything in it yourself. Once something is taken out, you have four options of how to deal with it, and none of the four options is to put it back in the tray. You will see what the options are shortly, when we look at dealing with paperwork.

If you're sitting back right now and thinking to yourself, 'Big deal. I picked up a piece of paper and had a look at it, I put it down and went straight back to the other job, and it's only taken me a few seconds', that's garbage!

It takes the average person between 4 and 8 minutes to get their thoughts back on track where they were before the interruption occurred. That's right, you can lose between 4 and 8 minutes every time you change your focus.

Remember you read earlier that people are interrupted in the workplace every 5–20 minutes. If we lose up to 8 minutes for each of these interruptions, that means that we could start the day off with a minus figure for productivity. And it could get worse as the day progresses.

If your answer is that you DON'T need to respond to the items put into your in-tray immediately, think about moving the in-tray somewhere else. Put it on top of a filing cabinet over in the corner of your office, put it on the table behind you, or better still put it outside the office altogether.

If you do need to respond to the items as they come in, then leave your in-tray right in front of you. You need it in front of you because you are paid to respond to the items as soon as they come in.

Your current work

You are probably paid to do things. So you will need some work in front of you! Not all of your work, though—only the project you are currently working on, your highest priority. You can't effectively focus on more than one thing at a time, therefore just do one job at a time.

As soon as you finish one job, put it away before you get the next one out. If you don't, there may be a tendency to lose focus, as well as losing information, because things may tend to get mixed up and lost on the desk. You know what it's like. Things get put in the wrong files and it's almost impossible to find them again later on.

It's a shame that most people only spend time cleaning their work areas before they go on holidays. They clean up so that they can go away knowing that they don't have any outstanding matters sitting on their desk. Why not do this each day, rather than waiting for annual holidays?

Beneath the surface

Okay, the top of your desk now looks really professional. Let's start working our way down.

We'll start by looking in the top drawers of your desk. What's in there? Pens, pencils, notes, staples, erasers, paperclips, business cards, old pay slips, last Friday's lunch . . .? Let's look at a couple of those items. We'll start by looking at the pens.

How many pens do you have in your top drawer? One, five, ten, twenty, forty, eighty, one hundred and sixty? Did you know that the average person has around thirty-six pens sitting in their top drawer? How many pens does a person really need? Only one or two, and maybe a couple of different colours.

I had a person on a seminar once who claimed to have between sixty and seventy brand-new pens sitting in their drawer! But that wasn't the bad news. The bad news was that they also said they had about six or seven pens in there that didn't write any more. I asked that person why they kept those old pens in the drawer, and do you know what the reply was? They said that the old pens might start writing again one day!

The average person has anything up to three boxes of staples in the desk drawers. How long will it take someone to use something like 30 000 staples? Certainly a bit more than a day and a half!

Some people even have boxes of staples in their drawers that don't even fit their stapler! Remember the day you went to the stationery cabinet to get a box of staples. You took the box back to your desk and went to put them in the stapler but they didn't fit. But rather than put the box back in the cabinet you thought to yourself, 'Maybe one day I'll get a stapler that takes these staples'. So rather than put them back, you put them in the top drawer of your desk. If you're grinning at this story you know exactly what I'm talking about.

The point in talking about pens and staples is this. Do you ever find yourself sitting at your desk working on something and find you have to stop, stand up and go and get something before you can continue on with the project? Most people do. And if I asked you why those items weren't around you initially to cut down on that wasted time getting things, you'd look around yourself and say, 'It's not here because there's no room for it'. The reason there's no room for it is that the drawers are full of rubbish!

I'll bet, when you clean those drawers out, you'll find many bits of paper in there and when you look at them you'll find you have no idea what they relate to or where they came from. People like to hang on to things, 'just in case I might need them later'.

There's nothing wrong with hanging on to things, as long as they don't interfere with your productivity. If you won't need those pieces of paper or those files for another 2–3 years, they do not go in the drawers at the side of the desk. They go in the filing cabinet way over in the corner of your office, or perhaps outside somewhere.

Keep up the good work!

Fingertip management is having at your fingertips what's needed, when it's needed. And the only way to do that is to move the things out that you do not frequently need or use.

Have you ever spent some time cleaning up your work area? How did you feel after it was cleaned up and properly organised? I bet you felt great! It felt like someone had taken the weight of the world off your shoulders. And what happened to your productivity after you cleaned up? It rocketed!

But then after a few days your work area gradually went back to the way it was before, and your stress levels started to increase. So it should be obvious to you that you need to maintain the organised environment. If you don't, it will take only a few days to go back to the old ways.

As soon as the paperwork and other items start coming back in, you need to prioritise them as soon as possible. Classify them as 'A' or 'C', or throw them in the bin.

The only way to implement fingertip management effectively is to move the things out that you do not frequently need or use. That way, you can bring closer to you the things that you do use frequently during the day.

Think about the location of your desk, your phone, your files, your computer, your phone books, your trays, your filing cabinets, and so on. Make the area around you support what it is you are supposed to be doing. Don't let it rule you.

Now review all the ideas you have from this section, turn to page 165 and write yourself another goal, or perhaps a series of goals, based on these ideas. Put appropriate time and date references beside these goals.

These techniques apply to other work areas also. If your motor vehicle is your office, for example, spend some time applying these ideas to the inside of your car.

Things will need to be put away some time, so why not put them away as soon as you finish with them? It will save you lots of time when you have to try and find the same item again later on.

You need to think about ways of putting things away so that you can find them again later on. This handbook will give you lots of ideas you may want to consider using.

When using your computer, use different-coloured labels on your diskettes to classify them. For example, you may use yellow labels for client proposals, blue labels for general correspondence, red labels for spreadsheets, orange labels for your personal information, green labels for your academic studies, and so on.

What are the things I am going to put back on my desk and in the drawers, or back into my workplace after cleaning it up?

_____

_____

_____

_____

_____

_____

_____

Sketch out the way you would like your work area to look (using fingertip management ideas).

When filing away paperwork or other items, think about using the same idea, this time with different-coloured folders.

Think about the things you use regularly during the day. Try and bring these items in closer to you, to save walking around looking for things. Which goals should you now put on page 165?

Fingertip management

 Fingertip management is having at your fingertips what's needed when it's needed.

NOTES

It's as simple as that!

If you have to get out of your chair, let's say six times during the day to get things from your bookshelf, and this takes on average 45 seconds to perform each time, then you are spending around 18 hours each year moving back and forth from the bookshelves. That's over two working days continually walking back and forth from your desk to the bookshelves! Scary, isn't it?

Spend money to save

You shouldn't be too concerned about spending money on resources to improve your effectiveness. If you were able to purchase some form of electronic information retrieval system to solve the above problem, you could be saving hundreds of dollars every year by cutting down on the movement time. For every minute or hour you can improve on, it's going to be worth money to someone. Look at the chart again on page 36 to see how much your time is worth.

How much is that 18 hours worth to you in dollars?

$ _____

Is it a good investment of your time?

This breakdown can also be used as a practical tool to justify allocation of additional funds or resources. If someone came to you and told you that, if you spent $400 on an additional office resource, it was going to save you $600 each year in increased productivity, what else could you say but 'Yes'?

Clean up your act

We can focus effectively on only one thing at a time. Everything we ever work with needs to be well organised, including our diary system, our kitchen cupboards and our filing cabinets.

Start by cleaning out your cupboards, wardrobes and drawers at home. Then move on to your message books, address books, filing cabinets and immediate work areas. As you start to clean things out you will start to feel better. You will be able to focus on the vital activities and not get involved in the clutter of urgencies currently around you.

Uncluttering the area around you allows you to unclutter your mind. Think of it this way. Every piece of paper on the top of your desk is another decision you haven't made yet!

If you have any ideas, write them down on page 165. Do it now before you forget!

Which one of these areas of clutter creates the most stress on you? Mark this one with the letter 'A'. Mark the other two with the letter 'B'.

Now that you have listed these three areas of clutter, turn to page 165 and write yourself another two goals. Your first goal will be to clean the area marked A within 24 hours of writing this goal. Your second goal will be to clean the two areas marked B within 7 days of writing this goal. Please put the appropriate time and date beside these two goals.

More goals

Here are a few more goals that you may like to consider for yourself.

Goal 1: No double-handling

Handle each piece of paper only once after it's been sorted and prioritised. Next time you pick up a piece of paper after it's been sorted and prioritised, you have one of four options open to you. These ideas also work with electronic paperwork etc. So what are these options?

What are three areas of clutter I need to clean up?

1.

2.

3.

Your first option is to FILE IT away so that it comes back later when you need it. If you work with a large organisation you probably have a formal records-management section in place already. That way, if you find you're halfway through a project and there are several files you won't need for a couple of weeks, you should be able to put your name on the front of the files, together with a return date. Some time during the day, someone will collect these files from you, and they will automatically return on the specified date. If you have access to this type of system, make sure you use it.

If you don't have access to a system like that, you will need to design your own personal retrieval system. For your own personal system you could probably set up a simple tickler file. This is how it would work.

You have probably seen slim cardboard concertina files in stationery shops. They usually have alphabetical tabs on top of the divisions. These are also available with numbered tabs, usually numbered from 1 to 31.

When you look at something and see that you don't have to do anything with it until the 10th of the month, you can then place it in the tabbed divider with the number ten. Using this type of system, you will need to make sure you open the correct tabbed section every morning to see what needs to be dealt with. This would then be included as part of your daily planning process.

By using this type of system you can defer paperwork to the correct date without having to rely on your memory to get things done. You should see fairly quickly that this type of retrieval system can be used for paperwork, invoicing, accounts and so on, along with numerous other applications. The only real problem is making certain that you look in the file every day!

Your second option is to ACT ON IT. Yes—actually do something with it! A lot of people overlook this obvious option. While you've got it in your hands, do something with it.

This may not necessarily mean completing the job in one go, but simply doing something with it. This could be just putting a note on the bottom, or passing it on to someone else for their comments before you do anything with it yourself.

Your third option is to REFER IT on to someone else for their attention. You can't do everything yourself. So is this something you should pass on for someone else to look after?

Your final option is to THROW IT AWAY. The priority level may have changed since you last looked at it. Priority levels do change. They are not set in concrete. What is seen as an 'A' today could be a 'D' tomorrow. On the other hand, what is seen as a 'C' today could be an 'A' tomorrow.

The only four options available to you next time you pick up a piece of paper are:

File it
Act on it
Refer it
Throw it away

These are the four options you have open to you the next time you pick up a piece of paper after it's been sorted and prioritised. The simple way of remembering the four options is simply remember the mnemonic FART. That's how to remember it, not what to do! Or if you don't like that word you could also use RAFT.

Goal 2: Sort your mail

You could consider having your mail screened and prioritised for you. If you have resources available to you for this purpose—and by resources I mean other people—make sure they have been trained effectively. That way you should see only the A's; your staff should be able to deal with the B's and C's, and they should be able to automatically trash the D's.

If you don't have people to do this for you, it's something you will have to do for yourself. But try and do it in the right part of the day. You should find, when you run your time log, that you have two highly productive periods each day (most people do). If your job has enough flexibility built into it, you should try to keep these high-performance times for the high-priority jobs.

You will probably also find that there are other parts of the day where your brain doesn't function at its peak, or doesn't function at all. These slack times should be used for the low-priority jobs or the routine activities. This is when you need to sort your mail, or do the filing.

Goal 3: Set your own deadlines

Sometimes, when people ask us to do things for them, they impose deadlines, and we try to work to these deadlines. Sometimes, however, there's no deadline imposed, or it's something we want to do for ourselves. If there's no deadline, we pick up the project or request in the morning and say to ourselves, 'It hasn't got to be done today', so we keep putting it off.

You need to impose your own deadlines. If you have a project to do for someone else or for yourself, and there's no deadline imposed, impose your own deadline. Say to yourself, 'I would like to have this completed by . . .'. By imposing your own deadline you will stand a much better chance of getting it done.

Goal 4: A clean desk

Have a completely clean desk or work area. Get yourself out of a reactive situation. Have you ever seen a very successful person sitting behind a messy desk? I certainly haven't.

Goal 5: Clean up before you leave

Clean your desk or work area every night before you leave. Many companies have clean desk policies. Why do they have them? There are generally three reasons.

The first, and most common, reason is for security. We all agree that we shouldn't leave confidential pieces of paper around for other people to find and read.

The second reason is for cleaning purposes. Some large companies brief their cleaners by telling them that if they find a piece of paper on someone's desk, they should not touch that desk. That way your desk never gets cleaned off properly.

The third, and most important, reason is this. If you clean your desk or work area before you leave, it means that when you turn up for work next time there is nothing there to react to. It means you will have to ask yourself what you need to do today. It gets you out of the reactive situation where you just do what you see next.

If you're sitting back and thinking to yourself that a clean desk policy is a complete waste of time because you're getting out the same things all the time, ask yourself this, 'Do priority levels always stay the same?' As we have already discussed, the answer is no, they don't. Priority levels can change dramatically overnight.

Eighty per cent of the time with a clean desk policy you will get out what you were working on yesterday when you left. But 20 per cent of the time you get out something different. So a clean desk policy is not a waste of time.

Goal 6: Get organised

Organise the areas around you more effectively. Think about the location of your desk, your phone, your computer, your filing cabinet and so on. Organise them so they're working for you rather than you working for them. Think about the location of your desk, your telephone, your computer, your trays, your filing cabinet. Are they all in the best places for you?

Fingertip management is having at your fingertips what's needed, when it's needed, and the only way to do this is to move out the things that you don't use frequently during the day.

If any of these extra ideas are relevant to you, put them on pages 177–84. And do it before you forget!

Typical time-waster 2:
Meetings

Have you ever walked out of a meeting and thought to yourself, 'That was a complete waste of my time'?

Someone once said, 'Meetings are where you get given minutes, but lose hours!'

Meetings can be a great time-saving tool or they can be one of our biggest time-wasters.

Current research indicates that the average business meeting lasts for 90 minutes, has nine people in attendance, and has an agenda only 50 per cent of the time. When it does have an agenda it should take only 45 minutes to complete, and in only 50 per cent of the time are these meetings completed.

As a participant, don't ever be afraid to set a time limit. 'How long do you think this will take?' is probably all you will need to ask.

Both the chairperson and the participant have responsibilities in meetings. Listed below are some ideas for both roles. These ideas will improve the use of your time in any meeting.

The chairperson's role

If you are responsible for chairing meetings, here are twelve things you may need to consider. You're probably doing most of these things right now, so this provides lots of reinforcement for you. Maybe, though, there are a couple of things that have been forgotten lately, so it's time to pick up these ideas and start using them again.

1. **Double your preparation time and cut the meeting time in half.** By doubling your preparation time this will help you (and probably the attendees) focus on the desired outcome of the meeting. It will then allow you to prepare for the correct parts of the meeting. While it may take you longer to prepare, it will save you (and the others) quite a bit of time during the meeting.

2. **Always use a written agenda.** As stated previously, only 50 per cent of meetings have agendas. If there is no agenda for the meeting, how will you know when all the business has been done?

3. **Allow participants an opportunity to contribute to the agenda.** By doing this you are creating a sense of ownership. With this sense of ownership there should be more commitment to make the meeting work, to keep it on track, as well as on time.

4. **Encourage participants to prepare for the meeting.** Getting participants to better prepare themselves for the meeting will allow discussions to be a summary rather than a full-blown discussion on the minor points. All the minor points should have been resolved before the meeting even started.

5. **Start and finish on time (or earlier).** It's the chairperson's responsibility to make sure the meeting starts and finishes on time. If a meeting is supposed to commence at 9.30 am, make sure it starts at 9.30 am. Even if you have only half of the people there, you still start at the allocated time. Don't punish the people who took the effort to get there on time by making them wait. Don't reward the latecomers by waiting for them before you start the meeting. And don't recap the points that have already been discussed during the meeting with the latecomers. Make them find out in their own time. These people won't turn up too late very often if you use these techniques. They will very quickly see how serious you are about your time and other people's.

    If a meeting is supposed to finish at 10.30 am, make sure it finishes at 10.30 am, or earlier! Meetings are allowed to finish early, but never late. Have you ever noticed how the task expands to suit the time available?

    On the other hand, we also need to allow flexibility. If the meeting is still going at 10.30, ask yourself the question posed earlier: 'What's the most important use of my time right now?' If you say that the most important use of your time is to continue with the meeting, then that may be the correct option to go with.

    Using a visible agenda also encourages a sense of urgency and helps to keep people on time.

6. **See that only the people who need to be there are there.** Don't try to create a power base by asking as many people as you can to your meetings. Only ask the people who must be there. If the meeting is being held just to disseminate information, think about sending out a one-page summary to everyone who needs to know.

7. **Assign someone to take minutes.** It's not the chairperson's responsibility to take minutes during the meeting. Someone else should be given the task. By giving this task to someone else it allows you to focus on your responsibility of making sure the meeting and its discussions stay on track. It also allows you to keep an eye on the time, to make sure that it both starts and finishes on time.

8. **Question the value of regularly scheduled meetings.** If you're holding a meeting today at 2.30 pm, and the only reason you're holding that meeting today is that you held it at this time last week, that's not a valid reason by itself to hold that meeting today.

You would be surprised at the number of meetings being held where no-one knew what the meeting was about. Don't hold a meeting just because 'we've always done it at this time'.

9. **Hold stand-up meetings.** A stand-up meeting is one where everyone stands up! Why do we hold stand-up meetings? Because they generally tend to be faster. Why are they faster? Because people are basically lazy and they want to go away and sit down. So use stand-up techniques to your advantage.

There are many meeting rooms around without any furniture inside them. This forces people to hold stand-up meetings. You may have held informal stand-up meetings in the past. For example, you've been standing there waiting for the lift to turn up and talking to someone at the same time. You may have been in the situation where you've said to someone, 'I haven't got time to talk about that now, but listen, I've got to go to the car park; do you want to walk with me and we'll talk about it on the way?'. That's a stand-up meeting on the move.

On the other hand, if you want people to be creative, have the people sitting down. People are generally more creative seated as opposed to standing. But think about using stand-up techniques to reduce the meeting times.

10. **Meet in someone else's office.** There are generally three places you can hold a meeting: in a neutral area, in the other person's area, or in your area. That is also the order of preference for selection.

By holding the meeting in a neutral area (the reception area or a meeting room) you can control both the content of the meeting and, importantly, its timing. If you think that the meeting has finished it's simply a matter of standing up and suggesting to the other person that the meeting has finished.

The second choice of location for a meeting is the other person's office. That way, if you think the meeting has finished, you can stand up and say, 'Well I guess I should let you finish off the other work you have here', and then walk out and back to your own office.

The last choice for the selection of a meeting is in your office. If you hold the meeting in your office, when can you start back on the other work that requires your attention? Not until the other person decides to leave!

11. **Pass information on to others in writing rather than in a meeting.** Always consider alternatives. If the only reason for the meeting is to pass on information, think about sending out a one-page summary of the information (or a fact sheet). That way it saves everyone's time.

Keep the information to one page or less for this reason. If someone receives a written document more than one page in length there is a tendency to put it aside to read at a later date. If the document is one page or less there is more tendency for the person to read it while it's in their hands. Try and keep all your paperwork to one page or less.

12. **Control the discussion(s).** One of the chairperson's major responsibilities is to ensure that the discussions stay on track. So if people start to go off on tangents, bring them back, and do it quickly. It only takes a couple of side discussions to take the whole group off focus. The chairperson must control all discussions and interruptions.

By offering periodic summaries the chairperson helps the participants to keep focused on the agenda.

What are three things I can do in meetings, as chairperson, that will improve my use of time and other people's?

1.

2.

3.

Participants' responsibilities

Participants also have responsibilities in meetings. If you participate in meetings there are things you too need to consider. Ten of these items are listed below:

Prior to the meeting

1. **Ask for an agenda to better prepare for the meeting.** Having an agenda allows you to properly prepare for the correct items. It also allows you to look and see if the meeting is relevant to your needs.

Asking for the agenda can sometimes have the additional benefit of getting the chairperson to sit down and prepare one. This can help them to improve their focus on what the meeting is about.

2. **Ask for the starting and finishing times.** Don't be afraid of asking for the starting and finishing times of a meeting. This allows you to plan around the meeting. By asking for the finishing time you can also create a sense of urgency in the chairperson. If you are asked why you need to know the finishing time, your response should be something like: 'I need to plan the rest of my day. There are other important things I need to organise'.

Sometimes, when you ask for the finishing time, it can get the chairperson thinking about your time. It's not unknown for the chairperson to rearrange the agenda to let someone go early because they said they had other important things to attend to. Items dealing with that particular person would be brought forward, and the other items put last.

3. **Predetermine the need for your presence in all or part of the meeting.** Ask for the agenda, or speak to the chairperson, to find out whether you need to attend the whole meeting. You may find that some of the agenda items have nothing to do with you. You can ask if it's possible for you to leave as soon as these items have been dealt with. This can also have the same effect as stated above, where the agenda might be rearranged by the chairperson to let you go even earlier. If they don't know, they can't modify it, can they?

4. **Prepare well for the meeting.** Preparing properly for the meeting allows for the business to be dealt with efficiently and effectively. That way there shouldn't be any need to explain all the minor points to everyone else. Everyone should have done their homework and been fully prepared for the final vote, discussion, and so on.

It only takes one unprepared person and one not-so-time-conscious chairperson for this not to work. If one person has not prepared properly for the meeting, the chairperson should not waste time explaining the finer points. It is more important to keep moving along, and perhaps suggest to that person that they had better prepare themselves for the meeting in future. Whether this is suggested in front of the group, or in discussion afterwards, is up to the individuals involved and the specific situation.

People learn quickly by their mistakes and this shouldn't happen on a second occasion.

5. **Recommend a recorder be assigned.** It's not the chairperson's responsibility to take minutes during the meeting. It's also not your responsibility! If the chairperson hasn't appointed anyone to take minutes, encourage them to do so. But don't volunteer your services, make sure it's someone else who gets the job. Unfortunately we have to be selfish sometimes with our time-management skills.

If the meeting is going overly long

6. **Ask: 'Is there any further contribution I can make to this meeting?'** By asking if there is anything else you can add to the meeting, you are

suggesting that maybe you could be excused from the rest of it. Or perhaps you should state it clearly. 'Is there anything else I can add to this meeting, or may I be excused? I have a lot of other important projects I need to spend time on.'

Another benefit of asking this is that again it can create a sense of urgency on your time. The chairperson may indicate that there is something that requires your input, but may decide to bring that item forward so that you can go and work on those other important projects.

7. **Ask to be excused.** There is absolutely nothing wrong with being asked to be excused from a meeting, particularly if you are really convinced that there is nothing else that you can give or receive by staying any longer.

If you think that there is nothing else to be gained from the meeting, simply ask if you can be excused.

8. **Open your organiser and do some planning or diary writing.** Have you ever walked out of a meeting and said to yourself, 'That was a complete waste of my time. I had nothing to say, nothing to listen to, and I've got nothing to take away from the meeting'? If that's the case, perhaps you could have come up with that statement before the meeting even started. That way you could have used the techniques shown above to ask if you could be excused from the meeting. The chairperson should have enough commonsense to realise you need not attend, and excuse you. Or the chairperson may highlight some point on the agenda that you have overlooked, and that will be relevant to you.

However, perhaps the chairperson will say, 'I don't care. You're going to come anyway!' If you are ever forced into attending a meeting that you know will be a complete waste of time, and you know that there's no way out of it, make sure you take your personal organiser with you. Then, when you turn up for the meeting you can open your organiser and start taking notes. Is anyone going to object to you taking notes during a meeting? No, they're not.

But what you're going to do is fool everyone. You don't open up at today's page and start taking notes about the meeting. What you do is open up at tomorrow's page and start planning tomorrow's activities. Or perhaps you can open up at next week and do some diary writing. Or perhaps you can open up at next month and start planning your holidays. Or perhaps you can go to the back of your organiser and start working on some of the projects you have set up.

It's really important we think about doing two or more things at the same time—but only when it's appropriate. If there is the slightest chance that someone is going to ask you a question during the meeting, you certainly mustn't get involved in heavy activities. But there is nothing wrong with listening with one ear and doing some light diary writing at the same time. That way, if someone asks you a question during the meeting, you will be able to come up with some kind of reasonable response to their questions.

9. **Sit at the back of the room and slip out when appropriate.** If you're attending a large meeting, position yourself at the back of the room so that you can slip out when appropriate. Obviously you can do this only if it's appropriate to do so, and if you have nothing else to gain from sticking around.

10. **Encourage the chairperson to use better meeting techniques.** By encouraging the chairperson to use better meeting techniques, it allows you to make better use of your time. The result should be shorter or more productive meetings, with less of your time wasted.

What are three things I can do as a participant that could improve the time I spend in meetings?

1.

2.

3.

If any of these techniques for making better use of time during meetings are relevant for you, turn to page 165 and write yourself another set of goals. Maybe it's appropriate here to use specific situations with these goals.

A quick test

Below you will see nine happy smiling faces. They are not put there just as a graphic to make you feel good! They are actually an exercise.

I'd like you to try and join all nine smiling faces with four straight lines, without lifting your pen off the page. It's important that you now take a couple of minutes with this exercise before going any further. Don't just sit and think about it. Get your pen moving. What I'm trying to do is see how things are working upstairs—in your mind, that is. Even if you've seen this exercise before, still take a couple of minutes with the problem. Every time you change direction, that's considered a new line.

What happened? Where did you draw your lines? What typically happens is that people make an assumption with this problem at the start. They assume that the answer is somewhere within the imaginary square formed by the nine faces. Wrong!

This is an exercise in lateral thinking. We need to go beyond the normal self-imposed boundaries we tend to place on ourselves. Sometimes we need to go outside the square with our thinking to get answers to problems. You will see one of the solutions to this problem on page 190. Have a quick look at it.

What typically happens next, even when people come up with a solution to the problem, is that they put their pen down and assume the exercise is finished. Wrong again!

When we find a solution, what we should do then is look for another solution, then another, then another. With this problem so far, there are well over 100 ways of solving it using the four straight lines. Even then we shouldn't be satisfied with that. We shouldn't say to ourselves, 'Okay, we now have over 100 ways of solving the problem using four straight lines. Which one should we use?' Maybe we should say, 'Okay, we now have over 100 ways of solving the problem using four straight lines. Let's see now if we can do it with three lines instead of four'. In case you're wondering, yes, it can be done. There are at least twenty-nine ways of solving it using three straight lines. Again you will see one of the solutions to this problem on page 190.

But even then, maybe we should say: 'Okay, we now have over 100 ways of solving the problem using four straight lines, and twenty-nine ways of solving it using three straight lines. Let's go all the way. Can it be done with one straight line?' Can you think of any solutions?

Yes, it can be done. A really thick pen could do it. That's just one solution. There are at least thirteen ways of solving this problem with one straight line.

The point of this exercise is to demonstrate the fact that we shouldn't be satisfied with one solution to a problem, and that we may need to go outside the square when we are looking for solutions to time-management problems.

When we look at time-management problems we need to come up with as many ideas as we possibly can. We then need to look at the quality of these ideas, but the quality should not be considered before we have the quantity.

It's possible that you may have participated in some serious brainstorming activities before. The facilitators at these sessions should encourage ridiculous ideas. They know that the ridiculous ideas generated may lead to more ridiculous ideas. They also know that the ridiculous ideas could lead to the perfect answer to the problem!

 The surest way to fail is to determine to succeed.

So—always come up with the quantity of ideas before you start looking at their quality.

Typical time-waster 3:
Overly long telephone calls

What do you do with the person who takes 3000 words to say 'Hello'?

Telephones can save us a lot of time. An average 3-minute telephone call is the equivalent of around 450 words, or almost two full pages of typed information.

Telephones can also waste a lot of our time. Imagine this situation. You have someone on the telephone. You've been talking to this person for a while now, and as far as you're concerned the call should finish. In other words, you've done your business and you've done your socialising. It's now time to wind up the call and start working on something else. The call started off as an 'A' but is now down to a 'D'. How could you handle this situation?

Here are some suggestions.

Use a time piece. It's amazing how much time we spend on a telephone call without really taking note of it. Keep track of the time you spend on each telephone call. You can probably cut all of them down. Have some fun at the same time. Use an eggtimer—the sort

127

with sand that runs through—to time your calls. Try and have each call completed before the sand runs through! Or when the last grain runs through, ask yourself, 'What's the most important use of my time right now? Should I turn the eggtimer over for another 3 minutes and keep talking, or wind it up right now?'

Use a monologue approach. By using short, sharp answers you are indicating to the other person's subconscious that the call is coming to an end.

Pose a spontaneous goal to yourself. A spontaneous goal is saying to yourself, 'What's the purpose of this phone call?' The spontaneous goal helps to bring you back on track. Getting yourself back on track makes it much easier to bring the other person back on track.

Use body language to wind up the call. How do you use body language on the telephone? Many people use a 'stand-up' technique to wind up telephone calls. If you stand up while you're talking to the other person it tends to create a sense of urgency. This helps to close the call.

Set a time limit to start with. Say to the person that you have got only until 2.15 to talk with them, then you will have to go to your next appointment, or whatever. Don't just say, 'I've only got 5 minutes to spare'. If someone says to you, 'I've only got 5 minutes', how long would you expect them to give you? Five minutes? Ten minutes? Twenty minutes? When someone says they only have 5 minutes to spare it's seen as a generalisation, so use specific times instead. Say, 'I've only got until [time], then I need to be gone'. Be specific, don't generalise.

Use a summary action. When you get to the end of the call give a summary action. This is where you say to the other person, 'This is what we've covered so far, this is what you said you're going to do, and this is what I said I'm going to do'. By giving a summary action you're effectively saying to the other person, 'Look if we don't finish now I can't go and do these things for you'. It's a powerful way of winding up.

Keep your calls short and to the point. Work out what it is you need to talk about at the very beginning of the call. Just try to stick to the point. This isn't saying that it's 100 per cent business all the time. We need to be social as well. Just keep it to a reasonable balance.

Track the people who waste your time on the telephone. By applying the Pareto principle you will find, by keeping track of your telephone calls for a while, that 80 per cent of your time wasted on the telephone will be caused by 20 per cent of the people you speak with. Identify these few people and look for ways of improving the situation.

Screen your telephone calls. Prevention is better than cure. If it's at all possible, have someone screen your calls. If not, you will have to do it yourself. If you determine that it's a low-priority call, get rid of it straightaway.

Tell the caller that you charge for your time on the telephone in 6-minute blocks. That may work if it's appropriate. Maybe you could say it in fun.

Be frank. Be honest when someone asks, 'Have you got a minute to speak with me?' If you haven't got time to spare, just tell them. Is anyone going to take offence if you're honest with them? No, I don't think so.

Ask a loaded question. Ask the caller, 'When are you going to pay your account with us?' That seems to move people along fairly quickly.

Hang up! This is the ultimate close. But as most people know, if you're going to hang up, you need to hang up on yourself. If you hang up while the other person is talking, they technically own the telephone call and they may call you back. Wait for them to draw breath and start talking yourself. Then while you're talking, hang up on yourself! You now technically own the call and the other person will wait for you to call them back. The call is a low priority to you and you obviously won't call the person back.

Tell them that you have to go to the toilet. The other person can't see what's happening on your end of the line, so paint a verbal picture for them. If you have people in your office or people waiting outside to see you, tell them. Create a sense of urgency.

Tell the person you have another call coming in. Even if there isn't one just then, this isn't a lie because when you think about it there will be another call coming in sometime today, or tomorrow, or next week. You're just getting ready for it early!

Always ring them—reverse charges. This is another preventive measure. Most people are dollar conscious. So this is one possible way of putting a dollar value on this time.

Use cellophane paper. How does this work? While you're talking with the other person, open up your top drawer and pull out a piece of cellophane paper. You can then start to scrunch the cellophane paper near the handset and say to the caller, 'I think the line is starting to break up, so I had better go now'.

Pretend the line has dropped out. If you're sitting there talking with the person and you're not prepared to be honest and say, 'I think I'd better go now', use this technique. When you've had enough, just say, 'Hello?', wait for a second, and then again say, 'Hello'. Wait for another second and say, 'Hello', and then hang up!

Obviously some of these ideas will work and some of them won't work. With some of your best customers and clients, if you know them well enough you can say some reasonably nasty things to them. You know these fairly blunt comments will get rid of them but, importantly, you also know they will laugh and come back again when they need to.

Faxes can also save us time and money. Although they take time to prepare, they generally get through more quickly and give a sense of both urgency and importance. To increase the likelihood of your fax getting through as soon as possible, try heading them something like: 'Please pass this on to [name] as soon as this transmission terminates'.

If any of these ideas for making better use of time on the telephone are relevant for you, turn to page 165 and write yourself another set of goals. Maybe it's appropriate here to use specific callers' names with these goals.

Overly long visitor stays

Imagine this situation. It's a similar one to the problem of the overly long telephone call. You have someone in your office. You've been talking to this person for a while now, and as far as you're concerned the visit should finish. In other words, you've done your business and you've done your socialising. It's now time to wind up the visit and start working on something else. The visit started off as an 'A' but is now down to a 'D'. How could you handle this situation?

NOTES

Here are some suggestions.

Keep the formal meeting tones in place. Doing this makes it much easier to bring things back on track if they go too far off on a tangent.

Set a time limit to start with. When the person comes in tell them how long they have. Try not to use generalisations, though. Don't say, 'I've only got 10 minutes'. Instead, say, 'I've only got until 2.35'. Use specific times. It creates a greater sense of urgency.

Stand up. Use body language to show that the visit has finished: stand up and start walking towards the door. You'll be surprised at how many people get up and follow you to the door.

Move the visitor chairs. Don't let people get too comfortable. It may be appropriate to use uncomfortable chairs in some cases. It may even be appropriate not to have any visitor chairs at all; leave them outside instead.

Use a summary action statement. This is a very powerful way of winding up. Say: 'This is what we've spoken about so far . . . , this is what you said you're going to do . . . and this is what I'm going to do . . .' By using a summary statement you're effectively saying, 'If we don't wind this up now, I can't go and do these things for you'.

Use appropriate body language. Perhaps keep glancing at your watch. You've probably seen people start tidying up their desk; perhaps pick up their personal organiser and close it. These things show your visitor that you're closed off, and make it much easier to wind up the meeting.

Have someone interrupt you. The prearranged interruption is a fairly common technique. Arrange with someone else (before your visitor turns up) to come in during the meeting and tell you that you have another commitment to attend to. 'Hey Les, do me a favour. I've got a meeting with Chris soon. Just keep an eye on the time for me. If the meeting has gone over 10 minutes come in and tell me that I've got to go and see Sam right away.'

Keep your meetings with visitors short and to the point. Remain focused on the topic. Don't let the discussion go off track. This doesn't mean that all meetings and visits need to be completely sterile. It's just suggesting that we need to have a reasonable balance between business talk and social talk.

Track the people who waste your time by visiting you too frequently. You will probably find that around 20 per cent of the people who visit you will waste 80 per cent of your time (it's the Pareto principle again). By finding out who these people are, you're halfway to solving the problem. Awareness is, in most cases, the solution.

Screen your visitors. Prevention is always better than cure.

Be honest when someone asks, 'Have you got a minute to see me?'

And for some of the more unusual techniques:

Ask your visitor if you can call them a taxi yet. For this option, you'll need to know your visitor well.

Get a couple of guard dogs.

Sit close to your visitor and take your shoes off. Maybe in some cases just getting physically closer to your visitor is all it will take to get them moving!

Flirt with them (but be careful, this could backfire!)

Use a really bad deodorant.

Walk out and just ask them to turn the lights off on their way out.

Again, it's obvious that some of these ideas will work, and some won't. You need to know the people you are dealing with fairly well. Once you understand them, you can start to develop specific techniques to handle different types of personalities and situations.

If any of these ideas for making better use of time with visitors are relevant for you, turn to page 165 and write yourself another set of goals. Again, maybe it's appropriate here to use specific visitors' names with these goals.

**Putting off an easy thing makes it hard,
putting off a hard thing makes it impossible.**

Typical time-waster 5:
Procrastination

The procrastinators were once going to form their own society, but they never got around to it. They kept putting it off! Sound familiar?

We need to stop putting off the important things. But, to do this, we need to keep putting off the unimportant things. So you can see there is a need for procrastination, but on the correct things.

The ideas shown below are some tips on how to avoid procrastination, but at the same time look at them for ideas on how to procrastinate effectively, so that you can keep putting off the unimportant items.

1. **Write a prioritised daily action list** every day in the 'To be done today' section of your personal organiser. Writing this list every day will help increase your motivation to work towards the correct things. You will be able to see at the beginning of the day how important certain items are. It can also create a sense of urgency with some of them.

2. **Make an unassigned action list as needed.** The unassigned action list is where we put all the things that didn't get done during the day—both personal and professional tasks. The unassigned action list helps you to avoid procrastination because it's to these items that we tend to direct our energies to avoid the other jobs. The unassigned action list helps to reduce the clutter of smaller unimportant jobs that tend to pile up around us.

3. **Refer to longer-range goals** when preparing the prioritised daily action list. This will tend to increase your motivation to work towards the more important tasks. Referring to your longer-range goals lets you see how important some of the tasks are in relation to the achievement of these goals.

4. **Cut the overwhelming 'A' into chunks.** The main reason why people keep putting off the important jobs isn't because they don't want to work on them or because they forget about them. It's because they look at them and say to themselves, 'I haven't got time to do that right now'. Why

don't we have time to work on these important jobs? It's because we simply don't have 4 hours to spend on one job in one go!

As stated earlier, most people are interrupted every 5–20 minutes in the workplace. That's why we need to break our 4-hour projects into bite-size pieces of about 20 minutes each. Breaking things into smaller chunks makes it much easier to do a little bit at a time. That way the whole job keeps moving along, and eventually it is completed, without too much procrastination!

5. **Make sure the high-priority tasks are accessible.** Keep the high-priority tasks close to you. That way, when you finish one job it's easier to pick up another high-priority job rather than getting bogged down on the lower-priority items that tend to surround us.

6. **Chain yourself to the tasks until the A's are done.** Stick with the job until it's finished. Sounds easy, but is it? It's too easy to put it aside for a short period of time, but it won't work that way. You need to stay with it until it's finished. That doesn't mean you can't get up and stretch your legs or go and have a cup of coffee. It means that after you stretch your legs or get your cup of coffee, you come straight back to the job.

7. **Anticipate interruptions that divert you from your A's.** Anticipating these interruptions also allows you to think of some solutions to them at the same time. Identifying solutions before they occur allows you to be fully prepared, should they eventuate.

8. **Involve other people to reinforce the A's.** If you involve other people, by telling them what you intend to do, it increases your commitment to work towards your goals. We don't like to fail in front of other people. Telling them what it is we want to do will increase our motivation to get these projects finished.

9. **Use a spontaneous goal.** Formulating a spontaneous goal is asking yourself why you're doing this job. Being able to answer this question should increase your motivation to get back into it, because you can again see the importance of it. Just ask yourself, 'Why am I doing this job?'

10. **Turn the difficult task into a game.** Most people enjoy playing games, so turn the difficult task into a game. For example, set yourself a challenge to get more done today than you did yesterday. Try to get more done this hour than you did last hour. Try to have less mistakes this time. Keep score if you like.

Bear in mind, however, when looking at increasing speed, you also need to consider safety factors, correctness, other people's needs and so on.

11. **Select the best time of day** for the type of work required. As stated earlier, when you run your time log you should find that you have a number of productive bursts during the day. Generally most people have two each day, occuring at much the same time. If your position has enough flexibility built into it, try to reserve these productive bursts for the high-priority items. You'll also find that there are other parts of the day when nothing seems to happen. These non-productive times should be reserved for the routine items: the ones that don't require too much brain power.

12. **Allow flexibility.** You must allow flexibility in planned activities. If you don't, it not only means that you could be dealing with a previously high-priority item that has fallen down to 'D' priority, but it also means that you can't allow yourself any type of break in the program. We sometimes need to allow ourselves a change in plan to refresh ourselves. As long as this is done for the right reasons, there generally isn't a problem.

13. **Commit to a deadline.** If you impose deadlines, there is far more chance that the project or task is going to be completed on time. So if you are doing something for someone else, or doing something for yourself, impose a deadline to work towards if one hasn't already been set.

14. **Use a reward system.** Let yourself do something that really shouldn't be done after completing a high-priority item. That could be allowing yourself to do a low-priority item that's been nagging at you for a while. It may be rewarding yourself with something tasty out of the refrigerator. It may simply be putting off your cup of coffee until you finish the project you are currently working on. Your reward is the carrot on the end of the string.

15. **Change the way of doing it.** Change the process so that it doesn't become boring. Think of new ways of doing things. We shouldn't always get stuck in the rut of doing things the same way all the time.

16. **Create a deadline.** When someone asks us to do something for them (the task in the delegation) and indicates a deadline, we try to work to meet the deadline. When someone asks us to do something for them and there is no deadline imposed, we tend to keep putting those jobs off because there is no sense of urgency. When there are things we would like to do for ourselves and there is no deadline imposed, we tend to keep putting those tasks off as well.

Think 'date and time'. Every function should have a logical conclusion by a certain date and time. Create a sense of urgency on tasks by imposing deadlines to work to. Without deadlines, tasks just keep going and going and going.

If you have an open-ended project or task to carry out and there is no deadline imposed, impose your own deadline. Say to yourself, 'I'm going to have this done by [give yourself a time or date reference to work to]. Create a sense of urgency against these items. That way there will be far more chance of their happening.

How do you eat an elephant? One mouthful at a time! Break things into smaller pieces. Do them one at a time, and all of a sudden the big overwhelming projects have been completed. And the funny thing is that when they've been finished they don't look as overwhelming as they were at first. Take one bite at a time, and suddenly you find the whole thing has been digested!

Typical time-waster 6:
Poor delegation

Why should you delegate?

- It extends results from what you can do to what you can control.
- It releases your time for more important work.
- It develops subordinates' initiative, skill, knowledge and competence.

How do you start?

- You need to work out the objectives of the task you are delegating. If you don't know exactly what has to be done, how will anyone else know?
- You need to ask yourself, 'Who can do it?' or 'Who has the ability to do it?' If it needs to be done straightaway, give it to someone who has proven experience. If it doesn't have to be done straightaway, give it to someone who has the ability to do it. Let them learn how to do it so that you build up your base of people who have proven experience.
- You need to work out how to deal with any personal or organisational barriers, such as tradition or refusal to allow mistakes. People make mistakes. Let them make mistakes, but only once! Obviously we can't let people make any mistakes in some areas, such as safety. But in some areas it's okay to make mistakes, as long as people learn by them.

There are seven basic steps you need to follow to delegate effectively. These seven steps are shown below.

The seven steps of delegation

1. Why

- Why is the job being delegated in the first place?
- Why to that particular person?
- Why is the job being delegated important?

2. What

- What should be achieved at the end? (These details will depend on the complexity of the job itself.)

3. Assistance

- Is additional training needed to do the job?
- Who can be called upon if help is required?
- What equipment can be used to do the job?
- How much money can be spent?

4. When

- When must it be finished?

5. Feedback

- Feedback needs to be solicited to ensure the person has fully understood the task.

6. Checkpoints

- Checks need to be made at pre-arranged times and places in case questions need to be answered.

7. Authority

- Tell others the task has been delegated, giving the person authority to act on your behalf.

Finally—do it with style! Develop your own style and use your own techniques. Don't make it a mechanical process. Each situation and each individual requires a different technique. Just make sure that each of the seven steps is covered in the appropriate sequence, and each is given appropriate attention.

Once we have taken care of some of our time-wasters and distractions, we can then start to look at investing some of that extra time in working towards our long-range goals.

Goal setting and personal values

Plan for the future, because that's where you're going to spend the rest of your life.

Mark Twain

If you decide to build a new house (which is a big goal in itself), you have your plans drawn up before any building work is started. This ensures that the job finishes up the way it's supposed to. Why not apply the same theory to other goals we set ourselves?

If you were to stop 100 people walking past your office and ask them, 'Do you have any long-range goals set for yourself?', do you realise only about two of them would say, 'Yes, I do'. Only 2 per cent of people have long-range goals set for themselves. Why don't the other ninety-eight people in every hundred take time to set goals for themselves?

Here are some of the more common answers that people come up with:

- 'I haven't got time to think about it.'
- 'I've got other more important things to do.'
- 'I don't know what you're talking about with long-range goals.'
- 'I don't understand what you're talking about. Tell me more.'
- 'None of my friends do it, so why should I?'
- 'It doesn't feel comfortable.'

There is often a fear of failure. 'If I set goals and I don't achieve them, am I seen as a failure?' There is also a fear of success! Yes, that sounds strange, but some people have a fear of success with their long-range goals. 'If I set a goal and achieve it, what do I have to do next!'

Another response is:

- 'I'm really happy doing what I'm doing right now, so why should I change?'

Why should these people have to change? Because they haven't seen the benefits of setting goals for themselves. So what are some of the benefits of setting goals for ourselves?

Goals help us to focus in on the really important things.

They help us to improve our lifestyle.

They help us to improve our standard of living.

They help to increase our self-esteem. How do they do that? If you simply set one single goal in place for yourself, and you start working towards it, what's going to happen to your self-esteem? It's going to increase. And as your self-esteem increases, what will happen to your productivity and performance? That will increase as well. It's a snowball effect.

They help us to make important decisions.

They give us a sense of direction. How do they do that? You may remember the story of *Alice's Adventures in Wonderland*. (We mentioned it at the beginning of this book.) Alice meets the Cheshire Cat, which is sitting in the tree, and asks, 'Cheshire Puss . . . would you tell me, please, which way I ought to go from here?' The Cheshire Cat says to Alice, 'That depends a good deal on where you want to get to'. What happened to Alice happens to most people. They come to a fork in the road, or a crossroads, and they really don't know which way to go. Unless we have clearly defined goals to work towards, it won't matter which way we go, because we're going to finish up somewhere. But maybe further down the path we'll realise it isn't where we wanted to be after all. It's like climbing the ladder of success and getting to the top, only to find that the ladder is up against the wrong building.

There are many reasons why we should set goals for ourselves. Most people simply don't see these reasons. Or, in contrast to Alice:

If you don't know where you're going, every road will get you nowhere.

Henry Kissinger

There are three kinds of people: those who make things happen, those who watch things happen, and those who say 'what happened?' Which group do you fall into?

Even if you're on the right track, if you stand still long enough you'll get run over. Everyone should set goals for themselves to make sure they don't get caught in this situation.

The first two letters of the word GOAL spell GO.

But what has been found is that, for people to set realistic long-range goals for themselves, they first need to work out their own personal values. Our personal values are the basis of the goal-setting process.

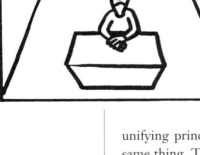

At the corporate level these values are generally referred to as the mission statement or the vision statement of the organisation. Most organisations these days have a statement of this kind, which should reflect the corporate values.

These values then help people to make important decisions in the workplace.

For example, just imagine this. It's now 2.30 in the afternoon and you're working on a minor office project for your boss or a colleague. You have a three o'clock deadline and there is still about 30 minutes' worth of work to do. So it's going to be a fairly tight deadline. Everyone else in your office has disappeared for the afternoon and you're sitting in the office by yourself.

Two people walk up to the front counter and are obviously looking to buy something from your company, or perhaps they're after some special information regarding your products. What do you do? Do you go and serve them and miss your three o'clock deadline, or do you keep your head down and ignore them so that you can meet the deadline imposed on you?

If your organisational mission statement says something about offering excellent customer service, or responding immediately to customer needs, then there's no decision to make. You respond immediately to the two customers.

You've now missed your three o'clock deadline. If the person who owns the project comes in at three o'clock and asks you where it is, you just tell them that two customers came in and you had to deal with them.

If this person then challenges you on your decision, they're challenging not you, but the values of the organisation. This is where we can use the mission statement from a decision-making point of view. That's also one way of using the mission statement for time management.

Now if that works for organisations, why shouldn't we have our own personal mission statements? In that case, if we as an individual get put in a difficult situation, we can then refer back to our own personal values and use them as the basis of a decision-making process.

Regardless of which term people use—personal values, unifying principles, personal mission statements, and so on—they all mean the same thing. They're something we can use to help make important decisions, and something we use as the basis of the goal-setting process.

Try the impossible—you may be the first to succeed.

So let's move into the first phase of the goal-setting process: personal values.

Goal setting phase 1:
Personal values

The first step is always the hardest.

A personal value is something we can use to help set goals and make important decisions.

Shown below is a list of personal values that someone noted down:

- to commit to a more excellent way
- to earn the goodwill of others
- to believe in people
- to have personal integrity
- to grow intellectually.

You may like these values and say you would like to copy them down and use them for yourself. But the chances are that your understanding of these values would differ from what was meant by the person who wrote them down.

Let's take an example from the list above: 'to have personal integrity'. So we're talking about honesty.

Imagine this. It's 8.50 at night. It's late-night shopping and the shops are going to close in another 10 minutes. There are only a couple of people shopping in the store, and there's only one checkout operator, who is way over the other side of the store.

You've just walked out of the aisles with a couple of items in your hands. As we said earlier, the checkout operator is over the other side of the store. You're walking over to the checkout area and halfway across you see a $1 coin lying on the floor. What would you do?

- Pick it up and put it in your pocket?
- Pick it up and give it to the checkout operator?
- Put your foot over the top of it?
- Pick it up and put it in the charity box at the front of the store?
- Kick it to the side and pick it up without being seen?
- Sing out and ask, 'Has anyone lost a $1 coin?'
- Leave it there?
- Glue it to the floor and watch the next person?

People will always come up with different responses. But let's change the scenario. It's not a $1 coin lying on the floor now, it's a $100 note. Would you do the same thing?

Some people would say, 'Yes'; some would say, 'Yes, but faster'; some would say, 'No'. Some people would say, 'I don't know, I'll need to think about it for a while'. Some may say, 'I walked in that way, it could be mine!' So we can see a bit of rationalisation taking place.

If we know what our personal values are it doesn't matter whether it's a $1 coin or a $100 note lying on the floor. Our personal values will be the basis of our decision.

That's not to say it will be what people actually do; but it will be what they would like to do, based on their personal values.

Personal values and priorities

Look at the diagram below.

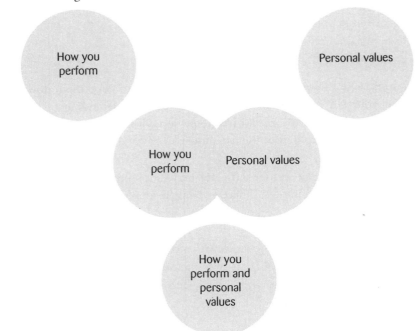

If our values and performance line up with each other (the first level, where the circles line up with each other) we feel pretty good about things. But sometimes our values and performance don't quite line up with each other (the next level up). And sometimes we have a significant difference between our values and our performance (where the circles are well apart). When we have this significant difference we tend to rationalise. Rationalising is convincing ourselves why it's okay for our performance not to line up with our personal values, for whatever reason.

The good short-term thing about rationalisation is that we can still feel okay about the things we have done, even though they don't line up with our personal values. The big negative thing is that people can lose touch with reality if they rationalise too much.

What we, as individuals, need to do is work out what our own personal values are. By looking at the diagram below it's easy to see that our personal values are the foundation of the whole goal-setting process. Without our personal values, everything is hanging in mid-air.

This diagram is a little different from most other ideas suggested by time-management theorists. Most use a pyramid concept, suggesting that one part is more important than the next. What I'm suggesting is that no one part is more important than another, that they are all in fact equally important, and all rely on each other. But as we can see from the four layers, it's our personal values on which everything is based. This is what the fifth generation of time management is all about—tying it all together.

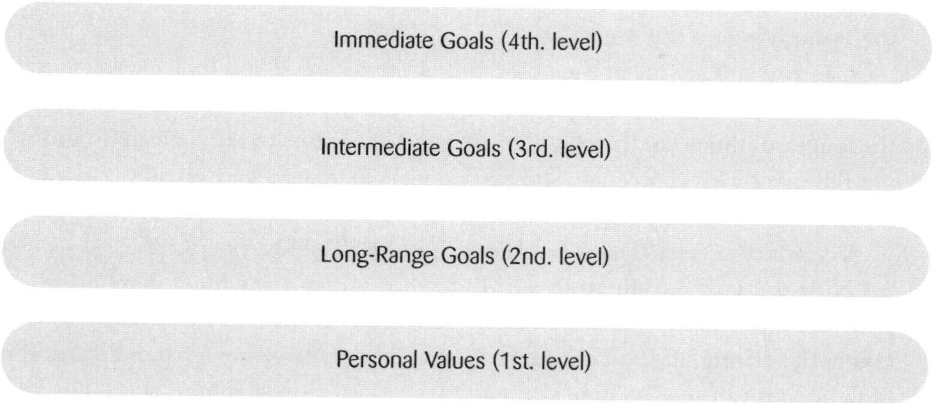

Immediate Goals (4th. level)

Intermediate Goals (3rd. level)

Long-Range Goals (2nd. level)

Personal Values (1st. level)

Each part links in with the others. Our personal values (the first level) are the basis of our long-range goals (the second level). The main reason people don't achieve their long-range goals is that they miss out on the third level (intermediate goals). Our intermediate goals are the things we need to do to either obtain or maintain our long-range goals. Once our intermediate goals have been established we can then start to transfer them across as immediate goals (the fourth level). The immediate goals are the things we do on a daily basis, and they build up to help us achieve our long-range goals.

You should now see a cycle forming. There is no start and no end to this process. It's a continuous cycle.

Visualise this

How good is your imagination?

Try and picture this. You are standing in a long narrow room. The room is 123 metres long (just over 400 feet). You're standing at one end against the wall, and I'm standing at the other end of the room. Can you see me at the other end? Now look down at the floor. On the floor you see a steel beam. The beam is about 50 centimetres high and 30 centimetres wide. It's sitting on the floor, so it's not going to move at all. The beam is half a metre short of touching my wall and half a metre

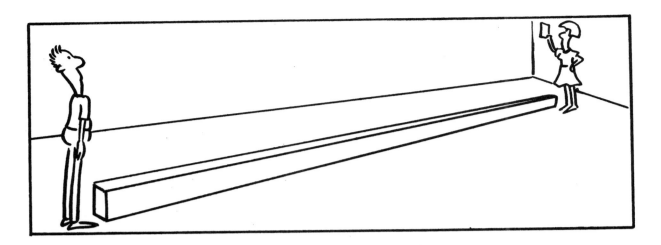

NOTES

from touching your wall. So the beam itself is about 122 metres long. Can you see the beam lying on the floor?

Can you still see me at the other end of the room? If you look closely you'll see that I have a $20 note in my hand. I am now going to ask you if you will walk along the length of the beam (on top of it) in less than 3 minutes. If you can do this without falling off, I will give you the $20 note! Will you do it? Remember the beam's on the floor and not going to fall. There aren't any catches with this.

I'm pretty certain that you will say, 'Yes, I will'. Most people do.

Now use your imagination a little further. All of a sudden a demolition company has come along and they are demolishing all the floors above us. They're just taking the ceiling off the 123-metre-long room we are currently standing in. If you look up you can see the blue sky and a few white clouds. There is a slight breeze blowing and you can feel the fresh air on your face. Can you feel the breeze?

If you look out through one of the windows at the side of the room you will see a very large crane parked on the side of the road. The jib of the crane is over the top of the room and the cable is coming down. The crane driver and crew have been asked to take the beam out of the room and take it further down the street.

At the end of the street there are two very large buildings. Both of these buildings are about fifty to fifty-five storeys in height. So they are both about 200 metres high. Can you see these two tall buildings?

It's estimated that these two buildings are around 121 metres apart. The crane driver and the crew have been asked to take the beam out of our room and place it on top of the two tall buildings further down the road.

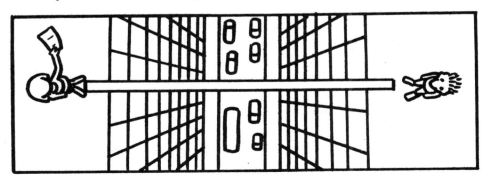

As they place the beam on top of these two buildings, you will see that there is only half a metre of the beam sitting on the edge of both buildings. There is 121 metres of beam just hanging suspended between the two buildings. A beam that size would be fairly heavy, so you will see that it's sagging a metre or two in the centre. The beam is 200 metres in the air, so there is probably a bit of a breeze blowing. So you should also see that the beam is swaying from side to side. See the beam swaying?

You have now been taken out of our room and placed on top of one of the tall buildings. I have been placed on top of the other building.

I'm now yelling to you across the void. I'm asking you if you will walk across the beam for the $20 note I still have in my hand. Will you? I doubt it very much! But they reckon that everybody has a price, so let's see what your price might be.

What about if I offered you $100 to do it? Would you? In all probability you would say no. What if I offered you $500? No! What if I offered you $1000 to walk across? No! Just imagine yourself standing on the edge of the building looking down. It's 200 metres down to the pavement and over 120 metres across to the other building! All you have to do is walk across, without falling off, to claim your reward. Notice I said walk, not crawl. You have to do it just the same way as in the room, no balance bars and no safety nets!

What about $10 000, $25 000, $50 000, $100 000? Here's my last offer to you. What about walking across the beam for $1 million, in cash! But, if you fall off, you've blown it! Even for that amount of money most people would say no.

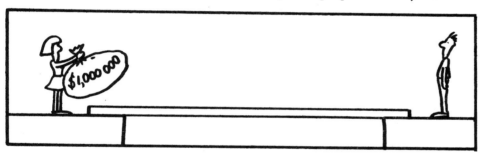

Now imagine this. I'm no longer at the top of my building and someone else is standing there. Now, if you have a child, imagine that child being held by another person by the ankles over the edge of the building! They now say to you, 'If you don't come across this beam now, I'm going to drop this kid over the edge'. What are you going to do now? You're going to go across! There's no question about it. In a real-life situation you would go across the beam to save your child, or at least try to.

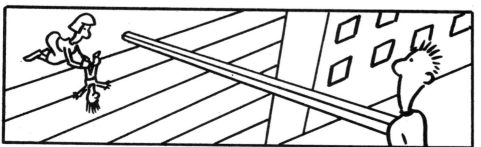

What does this story demonstrate? It demonstrates that we need to examine our values to allow us to make important decisions. It shows us that people do have values, and that some of those values have a higher priority for us than others do.

If we had a room full of money—let's say a million dollars—how much value would most people place on it? I would imagine most people would place quite a lot of value on it. But when we compare the value of someone's life with that room full of money, which one would have the higher value? The person's life generally would. And if we were assigning priorities to these values, the person's life would have the A priority and the million dollars would have the B priority.

When we then compare the value of that person's life and the life of their child, which one would now take the highest priority? The child's life would generally go up to the A priority and the person's life would slip down to the B position.

And where would the million dollars be then? When the person visualises their child being held over the edge of the building, do you think they would even think about the million dollars? No, they wouldn't. The million dollars in cash would go down to a 'DD57' in priority.

It's vital that we understand our values. As I've stated before, a personal value is something we can use to help set goals and to help us make important decisions. At the corporate level these values are generally referred to as the mission statement or the vision statement of the organisation. There are six steps involved in identifying our personal values.

Steps in identifying personal values

Step 1: Prepare a list of what you value most (your highest priorities in life).
Examples: honesty, self-esteem, family, humility, intelligence, leadership

To start with, you should find it fairly easy to generate a list. However, as you work through this exercise, you will think of other things that could be held over the edge of the building that you hadn't thought about previously. So you will probably keep coming back and adding things into step 1. When you have completed the bulk of step 1, move on to step 2.

Step 2: Write each valued priority as an action statement, and review them. What you are doing here is simply putting in some kind of descriptive action word with the values listed in step 1. As a result of this you should finish up with a list of statements rather than a list of generalisations.
Examples: be honest; have high self-esteem; love my family; be humble; grow intellectually; be a leader

Then, when we have this list of statements, we need to review them. While our personal values might appear to line up with each other, maybe they won't support each other.

Step 3: Write a paragraph of clarification under each personal value. Write a paragraph of clarification or explanation for each of the action statements generated in step number 2.

Looking at our first example in step 1, here is what the person may have meant by the statement 'Be honest'.

Example: Be honest with myself and everyone around me. Free myself from any form of hypocrisy. Be open and fair with my boss, employees, family and friends. See that justice is properly administered. See that all my business dealings are fair, completely above board and impeccable.

If you look at that definition and decide it's exactly what you would like to use, that's fine; you can copy it for your own use. However, some people may look at it and say they agree with most of it, but they disagree with the last sentence (maybe because anything goes in business). This isn't saying that one person is right or another is wrong. It's simply saying that people do have different values. And in some cases they may have conflicting values!

Step 4: Prioritise your personal values, using the 'ABC' system. Just like everything else in time management, our values have to be prioritised. But when you prioritise your values you will find that this is a little different, because all your values will be A priorities. You won't have any B's, C's or D's. So you need to prioritise your priorities, deciding which is the A1, the A2, the A3, and so on.

People often ask, 'What's the point in prioritising my values?' My standard reply is that if our values aren't prioritised we may be put in a situation where two or more of those values will be involved in the process. And if those values haven't previously been prioritised, it may make the decision on which way to go very difficult.

If we look at values concerning our family and money, it may be obvious to some of us which way we should go if a decision is needed. But, in other situations, the decision may not be so clear. Or you could regret a decision you made once you have looked at the long-term implications.

Step 5: Evaluate your performance over the past few weeks and months with each of your personal values. Once our values have been established, we need to sit down and compare our current performance with those identified values. If our values and our performance line up with each other, we will generally feel good about ourselves. On the other hand, our values and our performance may not line up with each other. If that's the case, it will lead you straight into step 6.

Step 6: Bring your performance in line with your personal values. This is the final step. You need to work out how you're going to bring your performance back in line with your personal values. But if you say you don't want to yet, all you're doing is fooling yourself with this whole process. You're rationalising.

Rationalisation is telling yourself it's okay to do what you've just done for whatever reason. The good thing about rationalisation is that it lets us feel okay about what we've just done, even though it doesn't line up with our personal values. The big negative, though, is where people rationalise about most things, or at least everything of importance. This is where a person starts to lose touch with what it's all about. Again all they are doing is losing touch with reality.

The discipline of writing something down is the first step toward making it happen.
Lee Iacocca

To start any process like this, think about the quotation shown above. Writing something certainly starts us off in a positive way on the process.

What are the things that are of highest value to me?

_____

_____

_____

_____

_____

_____

_____

_____

_____

_____

_____

_____

Now that you have started to think about your personal values you will need to set yourself another goal. Turn to page 165 and write yourself a goal similar to this: 'By [insert date] I will have written, refined and prioritised my personal values.' Be realistic with your time-frame; it may take a while to go through. If you have any trouble with this goal, ask someone close to you for assistance. Alternatively, there are many references on pages 194–6 that will assist you.

Goal setting phase 2:
Long-range goals

Once we have established our personal values, we can move into the area of long-range goals. That's not to say that it's impossible to set long-range goals without understanding our personal values. But without considering our personal values first, the long-range goals can actually work against each other.

First, what's a definition of a long-range goal? When I ask for this definition at my seminars, people generally say that a long-range goal is something that is a year away, or 2 years away, or perhaps 5 years away, or maybe 25 years away. My definition of a long-range goal is much broader than that. A long-range goal is as far into the future as you want to plan. Using that definition, a long-range goal might be something you want to do by tomorrow afternoon, or it might be something you want to do in the next 20 years. Using that definition, we aren't locked into specific times. It gives us greater flexibility with our goals.

If you had a goal of making a million dollars, you wouldn't simply identify the goal and then do nothing else about. If you did, nothing would happen. To achieve the goal you have to go a little further, otherwise all you'll have is a list of glorified New Year's resolutions!

'To make a million dollars.' Wouldn't it be better to develop that goal more like this? If you are now 21 years of age and would like to have a million dollars in your bank account by the time you retire at age 65, you would break your goal down. You would calculate that you need to invest $30 every week to have a million dollars in the bank at 65 years of age (based on 10 per cent compound interest). You can either do it this way or wait until you win the lottery. Which is the safer and more practical way?

So now we have our long-range goals established. What's the next step?

The main reason why most people don't achieve their long-range goals is that they miss out on the next level—the intermediate goals. And this next step is so easy!

 You must have long-range goals to keep you from being frustrated by short-range failures.

Goal setting phase 3:
Intermediate goals

(the action plan)

After we have established our long-range goals we need to get out a 'magic' sheet of paper. It's just a blank sheet of paper. I call it magic because it actually makes our long-range goals become reality. For every long-range goal we ever establish, we need to get out a blank sheet of paper.

NOTES

At the top of this page, write the long-range goal. Then list underneath it all the things you need to do to either obtain or maintain this goal. These bits and pieces are generally referred to as the intermediate goals.

Let's look at an example. As we all know, health is a very important part of good time-management skills. Maintaining excellent health may be your long-range goal. Obviously, before you continue with a goal like this, you would need to clarify exactly what you mean by the term 'excellent health'.

Once the long-range goal is fully understood, the next step is to put it at the top of your magic sheet of paper. Then underneath it list all the things you need to do to either obtain or maintain the long-range goal. These bits and pieces are the intermediate goals.

So what are some of the things you would need to do to maintain excellent health? Exercise? Eat the right things? Have medical check-ups? They're all right, but the problem is that they're not specific enough. The intermediate goals need to be very specific. So let's have a closer look at these examples. How can you make them more specific?

Instead of just 'exercise', how about saying something like 'exercise for 45 minutes every day'? That sounds much better. I'm assuming you know exactly what you mean by the term 'exercise'. Maybe it's jogging, walking, swimming or gym work. You must be clear about what you mean by the terms, or alternatively you could make the intermediate goal even more specific.

If you wanted to exercise for 45 minutes three times per week, you wouldn't just say 'three times per week'. Why not? Because there is no set start and finish to the standard week. It's not specific enough, and there is more chance of putting it off.

If you want to exercise three times per week, it would be better to say, 'exercise 45 minutes every Monday, Wednesday and Friday'. That way there's less chance of postponing it. Making it that specific almost sounds as though it's inflexible. It's not meant to be inflexible, but unless you have a really bad dose of the flu or your leg's covered in plaster, it's pretty hard to put it off. And if you do put it off, you have to make a conscious decision to say to yourself, 'I can't do it today for these reasons'.

What about our next example of 'eating the right things'? Again it's not specific enough. What about saying something like 'maintain a balanced diet'? That may not sound too specific for some people, but remember we are talking about 'maintaining excellent health', so you should know what a balanced diet is. If you don't, you may have to write another intermediate goal that says, 'see a dietitian before the end of this month'. Then you'll know what a balanced diet is.

So to expand our example a little further it may look something like this.

To maintain excellent health:

- Exercise for 45 minutes every Monday, Wednesday and Friday.
- Maintain a balanced diet.
- Have a physical examination every June and December.
- Have a dental examination every June.
- Drink eight glasses of water every day.
- Have at least one block of two weeks' holiday every calendar year.
etc.

Now it's easier to see how to break long-range goals down into smaller pieces.

Our long-range goals are the 'what we want to do' while the intermediate goals are the 'how to do it'.

Once these intermediate goals have been established we can then start to transfer them across as things to do on a daily basis—as immediate goals.

Goal setting phase 4:
Immediate goals

Now that we have broken our long-range goals down into intermediate goals, what's our prompt to work towards them each day? Remember the twelve questions we looked at in the preparation of a daily 'action list'? The first two questions were:

<code>NOTES</code>

- Of my long-range high-priority goals, which should I work on today?
- What will help me reach these long-range high-priority goals today?

That's your prompt to work towards your important goals! If you ask these questions every day and do a little piece each day, your goals will start to happen. They will become reality.

Let's go back for a moment to the question in the title of this book: 'How do you eat an elephant?' The answer is: 'One bite at a time'. By breaking things into bite-size pieces and taking them one at a time, things get digested. So the techniques used to achieve our goals are the same techniques as those used to eat elephants!

Each day we should ensure that we do something about moving a little further towards our long-range goals.

How to plan goals

If you fail to plan, you plan to fail.

When we plan goals there are, as a minimum, five things we need to consider.

When we read about goals we often see stories about successful football teams or other sports-related stories. As we said before, if someone wants to build a house they start with a plan. They know what the desired outcome is. So what about successful teams, organisations and individuals? They also start with a plan, and that plan includes SMART goals.

SMART goals are:

Specific
Measurable
Achievable
Realistic
Time-framed

SMART goals

Specific

Our goals need to be very specific. So rather than just being a vague idea sitting in the back of your mind, they are something very concrete. The best way to make them specific is to write them down. I refer to the type of goals sitting at the back of your mind as wishes or dreams. And how often do our wishes and dreams come true? Not terribly often, I suggest.

Measurable

Our goals need to be measurable in some qualitative or quantitative way (that is, to have so many completed, or to have it finished, and so on). If our goals aren't measurable, how do we know when we get there? How can we measure our success?

Achievable

Our goals need to be achievable—not too hard, but at the same time not too easy. We shouldn't set unrealistic goals for ourselves. If we do, all we're doing is setting ourselves up for failure. We also need to consider what success is. Is success actually achieving our goal, or is success simply working towards our goal?

We also need to ask ourselves, 'Who's help can be called on to aid us or assist us with these goals?' or, 'What resources do I need to work towards these goals?'.

Realistic

Are our goals realistic, or are we fooling ourselves? Check with other people on this one. They can probably give some good feedback as to whether or not they are realistic.

Are they within the framework of our personal values? Our personal values are the basis of the goal-setting process. It's pretty hard to sit down and think about long-range goals without thinking about personal values. It's also pretty hard to sit down and think about personal values without thinking about long-range goals. So you will probably find you do them at the same time, or very close to each other.

Time-framed

Our goals also need to have a time-frame. They need to be completed by a certain date, or we need to have so many done within a certain time-frame. If they're not time-framed they will finish up like most New Year's resolutions. That is, they won't happen. If our goals are not time-framed there is no sense of urgency to work towards them. The reason why most New Year's resolutions don't take place is that they didn't have a time-frame.

Why write it down?

People often ask why goals need to be written. There are many reasons, but the two most obvious are:

- because it involves a visualisation process (or realisation, or crystallisation)
- simply so that we don't forget what they are!

As it says in the Bible, 'As you believe so shall it be'. Here is a true story involving visualisation. It's about Conrad Hilton, the person responsible for all the Hilton hotels around the world today.

Back during the crash in 1929 people had stopped travelling, and as a result his occupancy rates in his hotels were down dramatically. In 1931 his creditors were threatening to foreclose, so many cutbacks were made, including the loss of some of his office furniture. During that year he came across a photo in a magazine of the Waldorf Hotel,

with its six kitchens, 200 cooks, 500 waiters, 2000 rooms, and its private hospital and private railway siding in the basement.

Conrad Hilton cut out the photo and wrote on it, 'The greatest of them all'. He placed the photo in his wallet. When he got his desk back he placed his prized photo under the glass on top of the desk. Every time he got a new and bigger desk he would take his photo of the Waldorf and place it again under the glass on top of his new desk. He was able to see the photo every day. Eighteen years later, during October 1949, Conrad Hilton became the owner of the Waldorf Hotel.

See it, believe it, achieve it.

To illustrate the second reason, here is a story about something that happened at a seminar I was conducting overseas a while back. A person towards the back of the room said they had a lot of long-range goals but they had them in the back of their mind. They asked, 'Why do our goals need to be written?' I said, 'Let me prove a point to you, but first can you tell me how many long-range goals you have for yourself?' The person thought about it for a few seconds and said, 'Yes, I can'. I then asked them to tell me how many. The person stopped and thought about it for a short period of time, and then replied, 'I have seven long-range goals', then quickly added, 'Seven that I can think of right now'. That was the point I was trying to prove. People simply cannot remember everything.

Something attempted, something done.
Henry Wadsworth Longfellow

An important question

When we look at our long-range goals we need to ask ourselves one very important question for every goal we ever set for ourselves:

Am I willing to pay the price?

For every goal we ever set for ourselves there will be a price to pay. We will have to find the time somewhere to work towards our goals.

So maybe we can't sit and watch television every Friday night. Maybe we can't go to the football every second Saturday. Maybe we can't play squash five times every week. Maybe there are certain things we won't be able to do at work. The time doesn't just come automatically. We have to find it somewhere.

But maybe the price we need to pay isn't as high as we might sometimes think. I just mentioned sitting watching television on Friday nights. How much time do you think the average person spends watching television each week? Five hours? Ten hours? Fifteen hours? Try over 20 hours each week! Recent research indicates that the average person spends more than 20 hours every week watching television. How much of that 20 hours would be really vital viewing time?

Even if someone could say they needed to watch all of the news programs, all of the current affairs programs, all of the documentaries, all of the sports programs, I think you would agree that there still has to be some 'D' viewing time included as well.

So for that person to turn their television off an extra 10, 20 or 30 minutes earlier during the day or during the evening, that isn't much of a price to pay! And now they have the additional time required to work towards their goals. Again this is not inferring that watching television is a waste of time. It's simply demonstrating that some people don't always do what they value most.

Another way of finding more time is to look at the possibility of modifying cycles.

Most people have heard the name Albert Schweitzer. But not too many people know much about him.

At the age of 17 Albert Schweitzer made a conscious decision. Up to that age he had slept on average 8 hours each night. At 17 years of age he decided not to sleep any more than 3 hours each night! If you know anything about him you'll know that he didn't sleep any more than 3 hours per night for the rest of his life. During this time he mastered four careers. He was the master of four professions: as a medical doctor in the jungle, as a concert organist, as a theologian, and as a philosopher. He was also a leading authority on the construction of organs and knowledgeable in anthropology and archaeology. How many people do you know who can make a claim like that?

Some people suggest to me that having so little sleep could affect your health. My response to that is: Albert Schweitzer lived to the ripe old age of 93. But then they come back and say, 'But he must have been bloody tired when he died!'

What am I suggesting? That you get up at 1.30 in the morning and start work? No, certainly not. What I am suggesting is that if you're like the typical person, who says they haven't got the time to plan their day or work towards their goals, then this could be one option available. Maybe you don't need to be as extreme as cutting your sleep down to 3 hours a night, but perhaps you could simply get up an extra 10 minutes earlier in the morning, or go to bed 10 minutes later each night. And use this extra time to plan or work towards your goals, not to watch an extra 10 minutes of television before going to bed, or to have an extra cup of coffee in the morning!

What suits the owls may not suit the fowls.

We must find the time to plan and we must find the time to work towards our goals! If you're not prepared to find this time or make the sacrifices necessary, then you may as well give up right now. Sorry, but you've got to give up time somewhere to find the time to work towards these goals.

When we look at our goals we need to break them into two separate areas: our personal life goals and our goals with the company. Because our personal life goals are more important to most of us, that's where we will look first.

Personal life goals

When we look at our personal life goals there are a number of areas, or categories, that we need to think about. It's agreed by most people that there are at least seven of these. They are listed below in alphabetical order:

- career
- family
- financial
- health
- leisure
- self-development
- social.

These seven categories are not shown in any kind of priority order. None is more important than the other. But they all need to be covered. You will see why shortly.

The seven areas

Career

Our career goals relate to the things we need to achieve within our identified career path. This involves identifying what career we would like to pursue.

Family

Family goals relate to the things we would like to do with our family. They may relate to the time we would like to spend with them, or the places we would like to go with them.

Financial

The financial goals show us what financial position we would like to be in. Some of our other goals can have a dramatic impact on this area.

Health

Unfortunately, a lot of people overlook this area. Without good health we may be unable to achieve some of our other goals, or we may need to modify them to take account of our lack of good health.

Leisure

Our leisure goals relate to the things we would like to do with our leisure time. Some people forget that we need to have leisure time. It helps to recharge our batteries.

Self-development

Self-development involves the things we would like to do in regard to our own self-improvement. They sometimes link in with our career goals, or our goals with our company, but they are independent of them. Self-development goals also help us to develop intellectually and spiritually, and they may help in the support of our personal values.

Social

The social category allows us to focus on the other people around us. Without social goals we can become introverted, and perhaps lose our friends. Social goals help to improve our relationships with people outside the family circle.

Yes, some of these categories will overlap, but that is to be expected.

What we now have to do is to write at least one long-range goal in each of these different areas. I say at least one, because if there's not at least one goal in the category, the category is missing. And that means that our personal life goals are out of balance.

Here's an example of what can happen if your long-range goals are out of balance.

Van Gogh syndrome

As a young adult Vincent van Gogh was a failure at everything he tried. He was a lay minister in the Dutch Reformed Church but made some serious errors, so he was removed from his pulpit. He proposed marriage three times and was turned down by all three women. At twenty-seven, in desperation, he picked up an artist's brush and began painting. His brother Theo owned a shop where he sold sketches and prints. Theo encouraged Vincent in his new endeavour, but with no knowledge of art Vincent's first efforts were rather poor. Eventually he left his home in Holland and travelled to Paris, where he spent time with some of the great Impressionists. Becoming disenchanted there, he moved to Arles, in southern France. There, in solitude, he developed his renowned style.

Having made the decision to become a painter, and not just a painter but a great painter, Vincent confided to his brother that he intended to do nothing but paint. Theo agreed to support Vincent until he began selling his work. In fact, he supported Vincent for the rest of his days, for van Gogh sold only one painting during his career, for the equivalent of $80 and in the last 6 months of his life.

We often set goals not to do things, as van Gogh did. When he said he would do nothing but paint, you might say that he was ignoring several of the basic categories for goal setting. While he focused on the self-development area, including extensive research in Far Eastern art, he ignored his financial needs and the needs of his body, often skipping meals for a week at a time to save money for supplies. He was becoming totally out of balance. It became an obsession as opposed to a passion.

With astonishing proficiency Vincent van Gogh could create a magnificent painting in an hour, yet at one point in frustration he sliced off a portion of one of his ears, put it in a sack, and sent it to a friend, a prostitute. He was confined to a mental institution for two and a half years. Ultimately within his 11-year career he produced 600 works, but at the age of 37, unable to handle the incongruities of his existence, he shot himself three times and died three days later. Had van Gogh balanced his priorities, he might have lived the long life of Pablo Picasso, who died at 92, leaving thousands of works.

Focusing on a single priority, to the exclusion of others, is sometimes referred to as the van Gogh syndrome. The workaholic suffers from the van Gogh syndrome, concentrating exclusively on the job, ignoring family and other obligations. This is not good time management.

You need to develop a plan that will keep you focused on the high-priority long-range goals, yet still take all seven categories into account.

Before we look at some examples of long-range goals in these different categories, we need to have a reasonable definition of what a long-range goal is. Remember my earlier definition?

 A long-range goal is as far into the future as you want to plan.

Using that definition, a long-range goal could be something you want to do by tomorrow afternoon. The next one might be something to be done in the next 25 years. Using that definition doesn't lock us into specific time-frames with these goals.

Some long-range goals

Let's look at a few examples of long-range goals in some of the seven areas.

The 'financial' category could include a goal such as, 'to be financially independent by [date]'.

The 'health' category could include the example we used before among the intermediate goals. The example given there was 'to maintain excellent health'. As we also saw, we can't just go and 'do' a long-range goal. These goals need to be broken into separate tasks, or things that need to be done to help achieve or maintain our long-range goals.

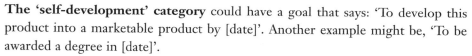

To maintain excellent health:

- Exercise for 45 minutes every Monday, Wednesday and Friday.
- Maintain a balanced diet.
- Have a physical examination every June and December.
- Have a dental examination every June.
- Drink eight glasses of water every day.
- Have at least one block of two weeks' holiday every calendar year.
etc.

The 'self-development' category could have a goal that says: 'To develop this product into a marketable product by [date]'. Another example might be, 'To be awarded a degree in [date]'.

The 'self-development' category may also have a goal that says: 'To keep my performance in line with my personal values'.

We should now finish up with a minimum of seven long-range goals. I say a minimum of seven because we must have at least one long-range goal in each category. If we don't, that means the category is missing and our personal life goals will be out of balance. Remember the story of van Gogh?

After we have our lists of long-range goals, don't forget the next very important step. That is to break them into intermediate goals, as we saw earlier. Each long-range goal should be written at the top of its own sheet of paper. It then needs to be broken down into the list of things that need to be done to either obtain or maintain the long-range goal. Again these bits and pieces are referred to as the intermediate goals.

What now?

Now that we have all these long-range and intermediate goals, what's our prompt to work towards them? Remember the twelve questions we looked at earlier for the preparation of our daily action list?

Question 1 asked: 'Of my long-range and intermediate high-priority goals, which should I work on today?' That's our prompt. And if we do a little bit of our long-range personal life goals each day, what's going to happen after a while? We will actually start to achieve our goals! Pretty frightening stuff, isn't it?

I've had people come up to me after my seminars and say to me, 'It really can't be that easy to achieve long-range goals'. Let me tell you right now that it is that easy. All we have to do is to identify our long-range goals, break them down into intermediate goals, and then start working towards them each day as immediate goals. It's really amazing what I've seen people achieve through this simple exercise.

 How do you eat an elephant? One bite at a time!

Let's look at your personal life goals. Write AT LEAST one long-range personal life goal in each of the seven categories.

Now that you have the basis of how to set your personal life goals, you need to turn to page 165 and write this: 'By [date] I will have written, refined and prioritised my personal life goals'. The date set for this should be shortly after the date for recording your personal values.

We also need to have balance with our goals. We can't just focus on our personal life goals; we also need to look at our goals with the company.

The seven categories for balanced personal life goals:

• Career (list long-range goals)

_____

_____

• Family (list long-range goals)

_____

_____

• Financial (list long-range goals)

_____

_____

• Health (list long-range goals)

_____

_____

• Leisure (list long-range goals)

_____

_____

• Self-development (list long-range goals)

_____

_____

• Social (list long-range goals)

_____

_____

Goals with
the company

Setting our goals with the company is just like setting our personal life goals. So this area should be a review of what we've just looked at.

What you need to do first is define the 'categories' of your position. The categories are the major areas of responsibility you have in your position. Just because I've shown ten spaces on the next exercise, this doesn't indicate that we all have ten areas of responsibility. Some people have nice, easy positions and they may only have four or five areas they need to consider. On the other hand, some people have very complex positions. They may have ten or twenty areas of responsibility. All the parts need to be identified, even the nasty parts of the job.

This sounds fine in theory, but how do we actually do it? Let's look at one example. Most people would be reasonably familiar with the role of a sales manager, so let's look at that position.

What is a sales manager responsible for? What are the major areas of responsibility in that position? A sales manager is probably responsible for the training of sales staff. So that's one area. The sales manager is probably also responsible for some of the financial aspects of the business—setting budgets and so on. They may also be responsible for the advertising or marketing of particular products. They may also be responsible for stock levels, or inventory control. And so it goes on. If you haven't been through this kind of exercise before, check your 'statement of duty' or your 'job description'; they provide a good starting point. I say a starting point because most job descriptions and statements of duty are out of date. While they might have been accurate the day they were written, the job changes on a regular basis. They need to be fluid descriptions and adaptable to change. Our roles all change on a regular basis and need to be reviewed frequently.

Now let's look at your position.

What are the major areas of responsibility in your position?

Position: _____

- _____
- _____
- _____
- _____
- _____
- _____
- _____
- _____
- _____
- _____

Now that you have identified the major areas, or categories, of your position, you will need to write at least one long-range goal for each of the different categories. If there isn't at least one long-range goal for each of the different categories, that means the category is missing. And if the category is missing, things will now be out of balance with your goals with the company.

The categories of your position:

[Category here; long-range goals listed below]

_____

_____

_____

[Category here; long-range goals listed below]

_____

_____

_____

_____

[Category here; long-range goals listed below]

_____

_____

_____

[Category here; long-range goals listed below]

_____

_____

_____

[Category here; long-range goals listed below]

_____

_____

_____

[Category here; long-range goals listed below]

_____

_____

_____

[Category here; long-range goals listed below]

_____

_____

_____

_____

Before you go any further with this exercise, I suggest that you now take these pieces of paper to someone you work for, or work with. Ask them to look at the pieces of paper and tell you if the categories you have noted down are your areas of responsibility, and whether the long-range goals you have noted are realistic for you or your position.

What you're doing is simply getting some role clarification. And that's important, because from a time-management point of view, it's pointless doing a job the right way, if you're doing the wrong job in the first place! We all need to know exactly what our job is and what's required in it.

After that person has looked at the categories and the long-range goals, and verified them, you can continue with the exercise. For each long-range goal you have written you will need to get out a blank sheet of paper.

Now write the long-range goal at the top of the page, and list all the things you will need to do to either obtain or maintain that long-range goal, or break the long-range goal into the intermediate goals. Yes, the procedure is the same as for your personal life goals.

So now you have all these pieces of paper with your goals with the company. What's your prompt to work towards them? Remember question 1 of the twelve questions that help us create our daily action list? 'Of my long-range and intermediate high-priority goals, which should I work on today?'

The question doesn't ask you just to look at your personal life goals. It's suggesting that you need to keep the whole lot in mind. That way you can maintain a reasonable balance of things around you.

That's it. That's your goals with the company. That's how easy it is!

Now that you have started to look at your goals with the company you will need to set yourself another goal. Turn to page 165 and write yourself a goal similar to this. 'By [date] I will have written, refined and prioritised my goals with the company'. The date for this should be shortly after the date for setting your personal life goals in place.

Once you have established your long-range goals (both personal and professional) you should then look at your plan for the year. You will then be able to see where these goals fall in and check them against other identified commitments.

A yearly wall planner or a set of yearly schedule sheets can be used for this. Look at the whole year and set aside time for annual holidays, weekends and so on. Now you can start to show major deadlines or commitments. This would include birthdays, anniversaries, training courses and so on. This overall plan should be accessible all the time. For this reason, a set of yearly schedule sheets in a personal organiser would be preferable to a yearly wall planner stuck on a wall somewhere, where it can go unnoticed.

Now set aside blocks of time to work towards your major projects and deadlines, both personal and professional. This would include papers to be written, assignments to be completed, projects to do at home and so on.

The individual tasks could now be highlighted with different colours. For example, your personal goals might be highlighted yellow, your family goals green, your business goals blue.

Then when you look at the yearly plan you should see an even distribution of the different colours. If there's not, you may need to ask yourself if you need to change a few things around. This technique will ensure that you have an even balance of activities when you look at the larger time-frame.

You should be able to see now that you are focusing on longer-range goals and values to help you work towards the important issues rather than just trying to deal with the urgencies that tend to pop up all of the time.

Most people spend the bulk of their day trying to prioritise the urgencies as they pop up. They just go around trying to work out which fire to put out next. That's only the third generation of time-management skills. We can now go much further by attempting to tie it all together. We need to work on our high-priority long-range and intermediate goals (the fourth generation), but we also need to have our hose ready to put out the fires as they start; we won't get rid of them all together. That's what the fifth generation is all about, getting it all together!

Summary of time-management ideas

You are encouraged to read through this list and select eight or ten goals, not previously included on your ideas list, that will be of the greatest help to you. These goals should be included on page 165.

NOTES

Preoccupation, alertness, energising

1. Make motions faster.
2. Do a job correctly the first time.
3. Locate energy losses, and fix them.
4. Establish a balanced exercise program.
5. Double your reading speed.
6. Do one thing at a time.
7. Use blank spaces in your time effectively. (Always have a high 'A' with you.)
8. Keep a writing pad directly accessible. Draw pictures and diagrams as you explain a point to visitors.
9. Arrive on time at meetings, appointments and scheduled events.
10. Reduce the over-long visitor stay.
11. Reduce the over-long telephone call.
12. Simplify everything you can.
13. Use your personal organiser effectively through customisation.
14. Keep your personal organiser with you.

Communication and attitude

15. Take 100 per cent responsibility when sending or receiving messages to see that communication is secured.
16. Consistently use sincere positive reinforcers on others.
17. Generate as little paperwork as possible—only what's appropriate.
18. Use positive reinforcers on yourself.
19. Try to enjoy what you are doing.
20. Remind yourself that there is always enough time for the important things. If it's really important you'll make time to do it.
21. Recognise that some of your time will be spent on activities outside your control. So don't get stressed by it.
22. Continually ask yourself, 'What's the most important use of my time right now?'

Delegation: boss–subordinate relationship

23. Instead of subordinates bringing you problems, have them bring you answers.

Meetings

24. Use proper meeting techniques.
25. Use stand-up meetings when appropriate.

Physical work area: organising

26. Organise your office using the ABC fingertip management system.
27. Clean your desk each day before you leave work.
28. Keep the desk completely clear of clutter. (Have on your desk only what you are working on.)
29. So far as possible, handle papers only once after they have been sorted; the same with e-mail.

Planning: daily

30. Take more time for systematic planning each day.

Planning: long-range

31. Refine all written goals, making them, as far as possible, specific and measurable.
32. Write personal goals within a balanced perspective so that they include the areas of career, family, financial, health, leisure, self-development and social. Refine and prioritise these goals.
33. Write subgoals to the life goals by raising the question, 'How can I cause each of these goals to happen?'
34. Revise your lifetime goals every 3–6 months.

Avoiding procrastination

35. Set a deadline for each task.
36. Do the most vital tasks now!
37. Turn the difficult task into a game.
38. Select the best time of day for the type of work required.
39. Allow some open space daily for flexibility.
40. Don't sit on projects.

Results: achieving with goals

41. Accept what you cannot change as a fact of life.
42. Use specialists to help you with special problems.
43. Use a visualisation technique.

Time-wasters and triviality: reducing

44. Say 'no' when a request is not vital.
45. Have a light lunch so you don't get sleepy in the afternoon.
46. Note and determine what routines might be changed to advantage.

47. Ask yourself, 'Will anything terrible happen if I don't do this priority item?' If the answer is no, don't do it.
48. Limit TV viewing to the 'vital few'.
49. Use a time log every 3–6 months.
50. Try to find a new technique each day that you can use to help gain time.

NOTES

Your assignment

(should you choose to accept it!)

What you need to do now is go through all the notes you've made in this book. You need to ensure that all your ideas and goals are included on pages 165 and 177–84. Once you're sure that they have all been included, you will need to go through them and prioritise them. When you prioritise these ideas and goals, don't prioritise them on the basis of time-frames. Instead, they need to be prioritised in order of importance. However, this order of priority won't necessarily be the order in which you tackle them. It may be that some of the low priorities will need to be done before some of the high priorities can be carried out, or it simply may be more practical that way. But don't use this as an excuse to keep putting off the high priorities!

This assignment could be the start of something that will change the rest of your life! You'll find that you will have the time to do the important things. You'll also find you have time for yourself. You'll start to feel satisfied with the things that get done. Your stress levels will reduce. The list of benefits goes on. In other words, you will start to succeed.

Perfect practice makes perfect performance.

What is success?

Many people think that success is achieving our goals; being able to tick them off the list. That isn't necessarily the case. There are many successful people who haven't been able to tick off any of their long-range goals!

So what is success?

 Success is the ability to identify goals and simply start working towards them.

There is too much happening today with the economy, with politics, at work and at home. There are too many people at the end of the football field trying to move the goal posts on us. Just because we can't score our goals, it doesn't mean we are failures. Simply working towards our goals is success in itself.

Why don't people become successful? Because some people don't have any goals to work towards in the first place, and because some people have fuzzy goals or just a vague idea of what it is they would like to achieve. Fuzzy goals lead to fuzzy results.

The ideas given in this book will help anyone towards success—as long as they are prepared to put in a bit of effort!

 Put nothing in–get nothing out!

The key
to your success

Who am I?

I am your constant companion. I am your greatest helper or heaviest burden. I will push you onwards or drag you down to failure. I am completely at your command.

Half the things you do you might just as well turn over to me and I will do them quickly and correctly. I am easily managed, you must merely be firm with me.

Show me exactly how you want something done and after a few lessons I will do it automatically. I am the servant of all great men and women and, alas, of all failures as well.

Those who are great, I have made great. Those who are failures, I have made failures. I am not a machine, though I work with the precision of a machine, plus the intelligence of a person.

You may run me for profit or run me for ruin, it makes no difference to me. Take me, train me, be firm with me, and I will place the world at your feet. Be easy with me and I will destroy you.

Who am I? I am Habit.

Ideas for making better use of your time

Ideas for making better use of your time

Ideas for making better use of your time

Ideas for making better use of your time

Ideas for making better use of your time

Ideas for making better use of your time

Ideas for making better use of your time

Ideas for making better use of your time

Ideas for making better use of your time

How to make your plan work

Let me simply use a few quotes:

The more I practise the luckier I get.
                              Anon.

If it ain't broke, you can't fix it, but you can improve it.
                              Anon.

What we have to learn, we learn by doing.
                              Aristotle

You have to build a bridge between now and what you'd like to be, like to do, and like to have.
                              Anon.

They just about say it all!

What is the
TIMETECH system?

NOTES

T	Tell yourself to set priorities.
I	Identify goals, both personal and professional.
M	Make sure you handle each piece of paper or message only once.
E	Exercise proper use of a diary.
T	Think to yourself, 'What's the most important use of my time right now?'
E	Every 'A' should be done before the 'B's and the 'C's.
C	Challenge what you do; challenge the system.
H	Help yourself and do it now!

If you think you are beaten, you are.
If you think you dare not, you don't.
If you like to win but think you can't
it's almost a cinch you won't.

Questions for preparing a manageable daily action list

- Of my long-range and intermediate high-priority goals, which should I work on today?
- What will help me reach these long-range and intermediate high-priority goals today?
- Which projects will give me the highest return on my investment?
- Is there a deadline to work to?
- Which project will be the greatest threat to my survival if I don't do it?
- Which project will be the greatest threat to my company if I don't do it?
- What projects does the boss want me to do?
- What wasn't completed yesterday that needs to be done today?
- What do my personal values suggest I should be doing?
- What does company policy suggest I should be doing?
- Is there anything else that may yield long-term results?
- What will happen if I don't do it?

Questions to help prioritise the daily action list

NOTES

- What will give the greatest long-term results?
- Which item will give the highest payoff?
- On a long-term basis which items will make me feel best to accomplish?
- Will it help reach my potential?
- Does it require other people to assist me?
- Is it a directive from someone I can't ignore?
- Which projects does the boss consider most vital?
- Is it important to someone I really care about?
- Will it really matter a year from now?
- What will happen if I don't do it at all?

Summary of five generations of time management

First generation	incorporates the use of notes and checklists to make sure things do not get overlooked or forgotten.
Second generation	incorporates the use of desk calendars, wall calendars and diaries to plan today's events and events in the future.
Third generation	puts the first and second generation together and also incorporates the use of priorities, personal values and goals.
Fourth generation	focuses on preserving and improving relationships. It looks at the concept of self-management rather than time management.
Fifth (and final) generation	ties it all together. It recognises that there are things we shouldn't forget or overlook, that there are reactive tasks that must be dealt with, that there are proactive tasks that must be dealt with, that personal values and goals are important to us, and that we do need to be spontaneous.

Solution to 'nine faces' problem

NOTES

One solution to the 'nine faces' problem using four straight lines:

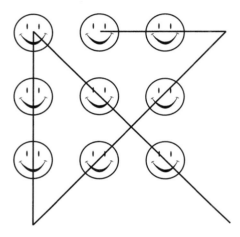

One solution to the nine faces problem using three straight lines:

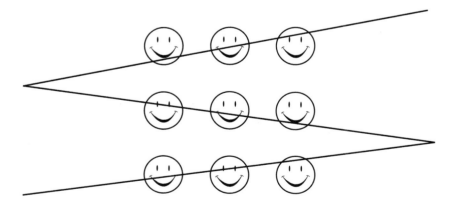

How many others can you come up with? However, before you start working on hundreds of solutions, remember the question you need to ask yourself: 'What is the most important use of my time right now?'

Top forty
time-wasters
worldwide

(not in rank order)

NOTES

Planning

1. Lack of objectives/priorities/planning
2. Crisis management, shifting priorities
3. Attempting too much at once and setting unrealistic time deadlines
4. Waiting for planes/appointments
5. Travel
6. Haste/impatience

Organising

7. Personal disorganisation/cluttered desk
8. Confused responsibility and authority
9. Duplication of effort
10. Multiple bosses
11. Paperwork/red tape/reading
12. Poor filing system
13. Inadequate equipment/facilities

Staffing

14. Untrained/inadequate staff
15. Under-staffing/over-staffing
16. Absenteeism/tardiness/turnover
17. Personnel with problems
18. Over-dependent staff

Directing

19. Ineffective delegation and involvement in routine details
20. Lack of motivation/indifference
21. Lack of co-ordination/teamwork

Controlling

22. Telephone interruptions
23. Drop-in visitors
24. Inability to say 'No'
25. Incomplete/delayed information

26. Lack of self-discipline
27. Leaving tasks unfinished
28. Lack of standards/controls/progress reports
29. Visual distractions/noise
30. Over-control
31. Not being informed
32. People not available for discussion

Communicating
33. Meetings
34. Lack of or unclear communication and/or instructions
35. Socialising/idle conversation
36. 'Memoitis'/over-communication
37. Failure to listen

Decision-making
38. Procrastination/indecision
39. Wanting all the facts
40. Snap decisions

Special
rush job calendar

Fri	Thu	Neg	Fri	Wed	Fri	Tue	Fri
9	8	7	6	5	4	3	2
17	16	15	14	13	12	11	10
25	24	23	22	21	20	19	18
33	32	31	30	29	28	27	26

This special calendar can be used to handle all rush jobs or projects. It seems that everything is needed yesterday, so this calendar will allow for things to be delivered before they are ordered. For example, something could be ordered on the 14th and delivered on the 12th.

Most things always seem to be required by Friday. So with this calendar there are four Fridays each week. This should spread the workload out a little better.

There is no 1st of the month with this calendar, thus avoiding late delivery of last month's last-minute panic jobs.

There are no Mondays or weekends, so Monday morning hangovers are abolished with this calendar, along with non-productive weekends.

A new day has been introduced: Negotiation Day. Negotiation Day has been introduced to keep the other days free for uninterrupted panic.

Two extra days have been included on this calendar to allow for the typical end-of-the-month panic jobs.

References
and suggested
further reading

Adams, Ramona S., Otto, Herbert A. and Cowley, Audene S. *Letting Go: Uncomplicating Your Life*, NY: Science and Behaviour Books, 1984.

Barnett, Lincoln. *The Universe and Dr. Einstein*. NY: Bantam Books, 1968.

Bittel, Lester. *Right On Time*. NY: McGraw-Hill Book Co., 1991.

Blanchard, Kenneth and Johnson, Spencer. *The One Minute Manager*. Fontana/Collins, 1984.

Bliss, Edwin C. *Getting Things Done*. NY: Charles Scribner's Sons, 1976.

Booher, Dianna. *Cutting Paperwork in Corporate Culture*. VT: Facts on File Publications, 1986.

Branden, Nathaniel. *The Psychology of Self Esteem*. NY: Bantam Books, 1969.

Carnegie, Andrew. *Autobiography of Andrew Carnegie*. Boston: Houghton Mifflin Co., 1924.

Covey, Stephen. *First Things First*. NY: Simon & Schuster, 1994.

Covey, Stephen. *The 7 Habits of Highly Effective People*. The Business Library, 1989.

Cranwell-Ward, Jane. *Managing Stress*. Hants, England: Gower Publishing, 1987.

De Bono, Edward. *Six Thinking Hats*. London: Penguin Books, 1985.

Deming, W. Edwards. *Out of the Crisis*. Cambridge, MA: Massachusetts Institute of Technology, 1986.

DePree, Max. *Leadership is an Art*. NY: Doubleday, 1989.

Dewey, John. *Democracy and Education*. NY: The Free Press, 1966. (first published 1916)

Doyle, Michael and Straus, David. *How to Make Meetings Work*. Chicago, IL: Playboy Press, 1977.

Drucker, Peter. *Management: Tasks, Responsibilities, Practices*. NY: Harper & Row, 1973.

Drucker, Peter. *The Effective Executive*. NY: Harper & Row, 1966.

Emerson, Ralph Waldo. Essays on 'Self-Reliance' and 'Power' in *Self Reliance and Other Essays*, Dover, 1993.

Engstrom, Ted W. and Mackenzie, R. Alec. *Managing Your Time*. Grand Rapids, MI: Zondervan, 1976.

Griessman, Eugene. *Time Tactics of Very Successful People*. NY: McGraw-Hill Book Co., 1994.

Hawkins, Kathleen and Turla, Peter. *Speed Read To Win*. Day-Timers, 1990.

Hobbs, Charles R. *Time Power*. NY: Harper & Row, 1987.

NOTES

Hobbs, Charles R. *Time Power Audio Tapes*. Day-Timers.

Kiev, Ari. *A Strategy for Daily Living*. NY: Macmillan, 1973.

Krannert, Herman C. *Krannert on Management*. Lafayette, IN: Purdue University, 1966.

Kroehnert, Gary. *Basic Training for Trainers, 2nd Edition*. Sydney: McGraw-Hill Book Co., 1994.

Kroehnert, Gary. *Basic Presentation Skills*. Sydney: McGraw-Hill Book Co., 1998.

Kroehnert, Gary. *100 Training Games*. Sydney: McGraw-Hill Book Co., 1994.

Kroehnert, Gary. *Timing Your Success For Students: How Do You Eat An Elephant*. Sydney: McGraw-Hill Book Co. (in preparation).

Kroehnert, Gary. *Time Tech*. Sydney: TECS, 1992.

Lakein, Alan. *How to Get Control of Your Time and Your Life*. NY: Signet, 1974.

LeBoeuf, Michael. *Working Smart*. NY: Warner Books, 1979.

Mager, Robert F. *Goal Analysis*. Palo Alto, CA: Ferron, 1972.

Mager, Robert F. *Preparing Instructional Objectives*. Palo Alto, CA: Ferron, 1972.

Maltz, Maxwell. *Psycho-cybernetics*. Englewood Cliffs, NJ: Prentice-Hall, 1960.

Maslow, A.H. *Motivation and Personality*. NY: Harper & Row, 1954.

McCay, James T. *The Management of Time*. Englewood Cliffs, NY: Prentice-Hall, 1959.

McInnes, Lisa., Johnson, Daniel and Marsh Winston. *How to Motivate, Manage and Market Yourself*. Melbourne, Victoria, Cassette Learning Systems, 1989.

McKenzie, Alec. *New Time Management Methods for You and Your Staff*. Chicago, Dartnell, 1975.

McKenzie, Alec. *The Time Trap: How to Get More Done in Less Time*. NY: McGraw-Hill Book Co., 1975.

Morton, Garry. *The Australian Motivation Handbook*. Sydney: McGraw-Hill Book Co., 1990.

Mosvick, Roger K. and Nelson, Robert B. *We've Got to Start Meeting Like This!* Glenview, IL: Scott Foresman & Co., 1987.

Naisbitt, John. *Megatrends*. NY: Warner Books, 1982.

Naisbitt, John. Abrudene, Patricia. *Re-inventing the Corporation*. NY: Warner Communications Co., 1985.

Odiorne, George S. *Management and the Activity Trap*. NY: Harper & Row, 1974.

Odiorne, George S. *Management by Objectives*. NY: Pitman, 1975.

Parkinson, C. Northcote. *Parkinson's Law*. Boston: Houghton Mifflin Co., 1957.

Peregger, M.I. *How to Chair a Meeting*. Brisbane: The Jacaranda Press, first published 1956.

Peters, Thomas J. and Austin, Nancy K. *A Passion for Excellence*. Fontana Collins, 1985.

Peters, Thomas J. and Waterman, Robert H., Jr. *In Search of Excellence*. Harper &Row, 1982.

Peters, Tom. *Thriving on Chaos*. NY: Alfred A. Knopf, 1987.

Rodgers, Buck. *Getting the Best*. NY: Harper & Row, 1988.

Schweitzer, Albert. *Out of My Life and Thought*. NY: Holt, Rinehart & Winston, 1961.

Selye, Hans. *Stress without Distress*. NY: J. B. Lippencott, 1974.

Selye, Hans. *The Stress of Life*. NY: McGraw-Hill Book Co., 1984.

Servan-Schreiber, Jean-Louis. *The Art of Time*. London: Bloomsbury, 1989.

Stone, Irving. *Lust for Life*. (Life of Vincent Van Gogh) Buccaneer Books, 1994.

Syntopicon. Great Books of the Western World. Chicago: *Encyclopaedia Britannica*, Vol. 11, pp. 896–897. (Some noteworthy philosophical discussions on time are by Pascal, Aristotle, Augustine, Locke, Einstein and others)

Thomas, Bob. *Walt Disney*. NY: Simon & Schuster, 1976.

Thouless, Robert H. *How to Think Straight*. NY: Hart Publishing Co., 1932.

Uris, Auren. *The Executive Desk Book*. NY: Van Nostrand Reinhold Co., 1975.

Valentine, Nina. *Chairing and Running Meetings*. Melbourne: Penguin Books, 1993.

Walton, Mary. *The Deming Management Method*. NY: Dodd, Mead & Co., 1986.

Warshaw, Leon. *Managing Stress*. Massachusetts: Addison-Wesley, 1986.

Watson, T. J., Jr. *A Business and Its Beliefs*. NY: McGraw-Hill, 1963.

Webber, Ross A. *Time and Management*. NY: Van Reinhold Co., 1972.

Whitrow, G. J. *The Nature of Time*. NY: Holt, Rinehart & Winston, 1973.

Whitrow, G. J. *The Natural Philosophy of Time*. Oxford: Oxford University Press, 1980.

Winston, Stephanie. *The Organised Executive: New Ways to Manage Time, Paper and People*. W.W. Norton & Co., 1983.

Wood, Evelyn. *Reading Dynamics*. Chicago: American Learning Corporation, 1988. (audio tapes)

DAY-TIMERS ORDER FORM

☐ Just send me a Day-Timer catalogue for now, thanks.

☐ Please dispatch the following items immediately:

Send to: _____

Position: _____

Company: _____

Address: _____

_____ Postcode: _____

Phone: _____

Fax: _____

Email: _____

Charge to: _____

Position: _____

Company: _____

Address: _____

_____ Postcode: _____

Phone: _____

Fax: _____

Email: _____

Products ordered:
Executive organiser—as shown in this book (includes: A5 size leather zip binder, 12 months' supply of dated daily pages, a full set of monthly calendars, 12 coloured tabbed dividers, special reference sheets, address and phone directory, 6-year planning pages, expense records, 3-ringed archive storage binder) $135 (Aust.) + $8.50 p & h

Number required: _____ Colour (black/burgundy): _____

Start month (Jan/Apr/Jul/Oct): _____

(Can start at the beginning of any quarter and will have the following 12 months' pages included)

Want your name on the front? ($5.00 extra) _____ (Please print clearly)

Note: A brochure will be sent with all orders to show additional items that may be used for customisation. Please allow 7–14 days for delivery from receipt of order. **Day-Timers offer a money back guarantee. If for any reason you're not happy with your order, simply return it and they will exchange it or credit your account in full.**

Payment details:

☐ Cheque

☐ Money order

☐ Credit card

☐ MasterCard

☐ Visa

☐ Bankcard

☐ American Express

☐ Diners Club

Card number: _____

Expiry date: _____

Signature: _____

(Please allow 7–14 days for delivery from receipt of order.)

See next page for information on where to send this form.

TRAINING INFORMATION

We offer a comprehensive range of training services around the world. If you would like more information on our training services, please complete the information below and forward it to us by mail, fax or e-mail.

Name: _____

Position: _____

Company: _____

Address: _____

_____

_____

Phone: _____

Fax: _____

Email: _____

I would like more information on:

☐ In-house Presentation Techniques Skills Seminar

☐ Public seminar information for Presentation Techniques Skills Workshops

☐ In-house Training Techniques Workshops

☐ Public seminar information for Training Techniques Workshops

☐ In-house Time Management Seminars

☐ Public seminar information for Time Management Seminars

☐ Public seminar information on other subjects

Post to: Gary Kroehnert
Training Excellence
PO Box 169
Grose Vale, NSW 2753
Australia

Or fax to: (02) 4572 2200

Or email: doctorgary@hotmail.com